D1552746

THOU SHALT NOT KILL

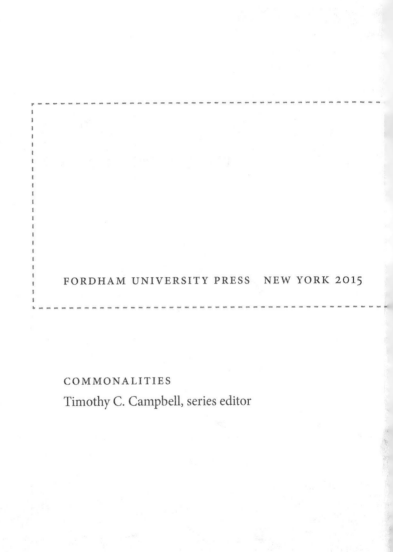

FORDHAM UNIVERSITY PRESS   NEW YORK 2015

COMMONALITIES
Timothy C. Campbell, series editor

THOU SHALT NOT KILL

A Political and Theological Dialogue

ADRIANA CAVARERO AND
ANGELO SCOLA

Translated by Margaret Adams Groesbeck and Adam Sitze

Copyright © 2015 Fordham University Press

All rights reserved. No part of this publication may be reproduced, stored in a retrieval system, or transmitted in any form or by any means—electronic, mechanical, photocopy, recording, or any other—except for brief quotations in printed reviews, without the prior permission of the publisher.

This book was originally published in Italian as Adriana Cavarero and Angelo Scola, *Non Uccidere*, © 2011 by Società editrice il Mulino, Bologna.

The translation of this work has been funded by SEPS
Segretariato Europeo per le Pubblicazioni Scientifiche

S E P S

Via Val d'Aposa 7 - 40123 Bologna - Italy
seps@seps.it - www.seps.it

Fordham University Press has no responsibility for the persistence or accuracy of URLs for external or third-party Internet websites referred to in this publication and does not guarantee that any content on such websites is, or will remain, accurate or appropriate.

Fordham University Press also publishes its books in a variety of electronic formats. Some content that appears in print may not be available in electronic books.

Visit us online at www.fordhampress.com.

Library of Congress Cataloging-in-Publication Data

Cavarero, Adriana.
   [Non uccidere. English]
   Thou shalt not kill : a political and theological dialogue /
Adriana Cavarero and Angelo Scola ; translated by Margaret
Adams Groesbeck and Adam Sitze.—First edition.
     pages cm. — (Commonalities)
   Includes bibliographical references and index.
   ISBN 978-0-8232-6734-7 (cloth : alk. paper) —
   ISBN 978-0-8232-6735-4 (pbk. : alk. paper)
  1. Ten commandments—Murder.   I. Scola, Angelo.
II. Title.
   BV4680.C3813 2015
   179.7—dc23

                                 2015009512

Printed in the United States of America
17 16 15   5 4 3 2 1
First edition

CONTENTS

TRANSLATORS' NOTE

The translators express gratitude for the invaluable help and support of Steve Heim, Brian Ingram, Bongani Ndlovu, Susan Stinson, and Steven Stover.

POINT OF DEPARTURE

Whosoever destroys one man is counted by Scripture as though he had destroyed the whole world. This is also true of Cain who killed Abel, his brother, as it is written in the Scripture: *The voice of thy brother's blood crieth unto Me* (Genesis 4.10). Though he may shed the blood (*dm*) of only a single person, the text uses the plural: *dmym* ("bloods"). This teaches us that the blood of Abel's children, and his children's children, and all the descendants destined to come forth from him until the end of time—all of them stood crying out before the Holy One, blessed be He. Thus thou dost learn that one man's life is equal to all the work of creation.[1]

This important affirmation, to which we could add others with similar and even more radical importance, would suffice to demonstrate the need to place the commandment "You shall not kill" in its original context and to highlight what Christian tradition, passed down through Western culture, recognizes in the commandment.

We should point out right away what *The Catechism of the Catholic Church* reminds us:

> The division and numbering of the Commandments have varied in the course of history. The present catechism follows the division of the Commandments established by St. Augustine, which has become traditional in the Catholic Church. It is also that of the Lutheran confessions. The Greek Fathers worked out a slightly different division, which is found in the Orthodox Churches and Reformed communities.[2]

For this reason it is worth giving a synopsis of the Hebrew division of the "ten words"[3] and that of the Ten Commandments of the Catechism (see accompanying table).[4]

The contextualization of these "ten words," which if done fully would require enormous effort, allows us to reveal the deeper meaning proper to their formulation in the book of Exodus, to which the passage of time has grafted other values that sometimes have changed more than just the words' literal meaning.

If, for example, we refer to some recent Jewish commentaries on Exodus 20, which contains the "ten words"—among them "You shall not kill"[5]—we learn that the root of the term used here directly refers only to

Exodus 20.2–17	Deuteronomy 5.6–21	Catholic Formula
I am Yahweh your God who brought you out of the land of Egypt, out of the house of slavery.	I am Yahweh your God who brought you out of the land of Egypt, out of the house of slavery.	I am the LORD your God: you shall not have strange Gods before me.
You shall have no gods except me. You shall not make yourself a carved image or any likeness of anything in heaven or on earth beneath or in the waters under the earth; you shall not bow down to them or serve them. For I, Yahweh your God, am a jealous God and I punish the father's fault in the sons, the grandsons, and the great-grandsons of those who hate me; but I show kindness to thousands of those who love me and keep my commandments.	You shall have no gods except me . . .	
You shall not utter the name of Yahweh your God to misuse it, for Yahweh will not leave unpunished the man who utters his name to misuse it.	You shall not utter the name of Yahweh your God to misuse it . . .	You shall not take the name of the LORD your God in vain.

(Continued) |

Exodus 20.2–17	Deuteronomy 5.6–21	Catholic Formula
Remember the Sabbath day and keep it holy. For six days you shall labour and do all your work, but the seventh day is a Sabbath for Yahweh your God. You shall do no work that day, neither you nor your son nor your daughter nor your servants, men or women, nor your animals nor the stranger who lives with you. For six days Yahweh made the heavens and the earth and the sea and all that these hold, but on the seventh day he rested; that is why Yahweh has blessed the Sabbath and made it sacred.	Observe the Sabbath day and keep it holy . . .	Remember to keep holy the LORD's Day.
Honour your father and your mother so that you may have a long life in the land that Yahweh your God has given you.	Honour your father and your mother . . .	Honor your father and your mother.
You shall not kill.	You shall not kill.	You shall not kill.
You shall not commit adultery.	You shall not commit adultery.	You shall not commit adultery.

You shall not steal.	You shall not steal.	You shall not steal.
You shall not bear false witness against your neighbor.	You shall not bear false witness against your neighbor.	You shall not bear false witness against your neighbor.
You shall not covet your neighbor's house. You shall not covet your neighbor's wife, or his servant, man or woman, or his ox, or his donkey, or anything that is his.	You shall not covet your neighbor's wife, you shall not set your heart on his house, his field, his servant—man or woman—his ox, his donkey, or anything that is his.	You shall not covet your neighbor's wife.
	You shall not set your heart on his house, his field, his servant—man or woman—his ox, his donkey, or anything that is his.	You shall not covet your neighbor's goods.

unjustified killing. And it must be placed in a wider context, supported by still other sources,[6] to enable us to assert that, with the word "You shall not kill," God asks that we "not, therefore vandalize My creation by spilling human blood, for I created human beings to honor and acknowledge Me in all these ways."[7] This lets more than one commentator maintain that, since the text of Exodus 20 refers only to "unauthorized homicide," it cannot by itself be used to exclude "killing during war" or to support the "abolition of capital punishment." Following this reasoning, one would remain unable to derive from this commandment a "prohibition against suicide."[8]

To offer a last significant example, another well-known commentator asserts that "strictly speaking, other acts such as idolatry, Sabbath violation, and sexual crimes are considered more significant than murder because they are crimes against God and not crimes against man, as is murder."[9]

Obviously these remarks are not intended to diminish the import or radical qualities of "You shall not kill." They instead aim to free the commandment from an ahistorical vision that makes it refer to an abstract universal—a vision that has been widespread from the Enlightenment on and that holds that the religious roots for any principle—such as the commandments are when considered in their objective mode—are bound to history, "regionalizing" those roots in a way that deprives them of their universal force. In fact, the concrete universals of religion avoid the abstraction of any purely theoretical affirmation of principles. Abstractions such as these, incidentally, are in no small way responsible for the extreme difficulties that current democracies, founded though they may be on agreed-upon procedures, experience whenever they try to reach "grand compromises" that will guarantee a good life, even in a pluralist society.[10]

In order to better situate our theme, let us offer a last brief comment on the Christian interpretation of the Ten Commandments.

First of all, recent Christian commentators agree in recognizing that the special character of the Decalogue, not the least of which is the lack of an object in commandments 5 through 7,[11] has encouraged throughout history a reading of the Ten Commandments as a collection of precepts outside of time, as a set of immutable divine laws. More careful studies, as we shall see, rightly have gone beyond that reductive position to read the commandments narrowly within the context of the Covenant of Sinai. This permits them, in turn, to be understood as correlates to the living will of God, where the Ten Commandments deal always with His manifestation: "I am Yahweh." On one hand, this means that the commandments are not reducible to something purely adaptable to every historical moment. On the other, however, the Decalogue demands different applications as history moves along. Both the absoluteness of the Decalogue and, at the same time, its bond with history are thus guaranteed, and it is none other than this close relationship with the living God—with the God of the covenant who always asks of his people fidelity and renewal—that provides this guarantee.[12]

Whatever the exact meaning of the commandment under review, the Christian exegesis hardly moves far from the Jewish one, to which it often makes specific reference. In substance it recognizes a progressive evolution from an originary level bound to voluntary homicide in order to save the innocent, to assume, little by little, the character of a condemnation of every act of violence against another that stems from feelings of hatred or ill will. The commandment finally reaches the point of excluding the pretext of rendering justice by oneself, even when one suffers an objective, serious injustice.[13]

At this point it might be useful to recall, from a dialogue between André LaCocque and Paul Ricoeur, a telling observation on the relationship between this commandment and the entire corpus of the Bible.[14] There LaCocque highlights the tension between "You shall not kill" and the divine demand that Abraham sacrifice his son.[15] On one hand, in this way, the fifth commandment is set in relation to the first (to honor Yahweh): "You shall not kill" indicates the absolute, unconditional worth of human life. But, on the other hand, departing from a Kierkegaardian reading of the interrupted sacrifice of Isaac, it seems to LaCocque to be able to annul the "You shall not kill" in a "narrative and prescriptive" way. In the divine claim on Abraham's first born, the scholar believes he is singling out a new limitation on the commandment, one besides those condemning war and capital punishment. We would be dealing with what Kierkegaard called a "teleological suspension of the ethical"[16]—that is, with a suspension of the commandment's apodictic character that, in turn, would reveal the existence of a metaethic internal to the Bible itself. Ricoeur's answer to this questionable interpretation is both profound and precise. The relation between Genesis 22 and the commandment "You shall not kill," he says, should be read starting not from the *exception* but rather from the *excess* of love in relation to justice.[17]

COMMANDMENTS
AND COVENANT

This introductory framework should suffice to demonstrate that the very concept of "commandment," when linked to the precepts of the Decalogue, requires a clarification that restates the authentic law. If we are to grasp the meanings of moral law in its actual cultural context, we cannot possibly trust some sort of common sense without immediately getting lost in a maze of multiple misunderstandings and contradictions. We will have to find ways to peel off the sedimented crust formed by the usual meanings and to strip ambiguity from the very debates that should have critically illuminated the problems.

Unavoidably, therefore, if the meaning of the commandments is not to be distorted, it becomes necessary to situate them, whether taken individually or all together, in the general context of the Bible. If we understand them not as the "ten words" of God but instead as the command of an imperative will, we misrepresent their meaning, whether from the point of view of content or that of method. Influenced by late medieval and modern voluntarism, we immediately read the commandments as imperatives from an authority who is at once absolute, vertical, and exterior.

The Decalogue cannot, however, be separated from the historical covenant God establishes with the people of Israel and, through them, with all humanity. The Decalogue is offered and "written on two stone tablets" in a clearly defined historical circumstance, and it cannot in any way be taken out of the close association with the divine action through which it was given. It cannot be idealistically, moralistically, or spiritually extrapolated from holy history and represented, in an Enlightenment manner, as some kind of canon based on an abstract universalism.

The substance of the "ten words" consists in their being an expression of the covenant. For just this reason the tablets will be set inside the Ark of the Covenant: to demonstrate that it is the *embrace* [*comprehensor*] in which the "ten words" remain. The "ten words" say for certain that there is no covenant without a content, but they also demonstrate that it is not that content that institutes and grounds it.

The "ten words" therefore always refer back to the relation of the covenant established by God with his chosen People as the grounds for their originary law. The principles that "We will observe" and "We will obey"[1] are always premised on the action of God, who has given us freedom, who has liberated us, showing us a path and giving us the strength to continue following it. Therefore the end of every "doing" and "observing" is the relation with Him, is He Himself. The covenant in Sinai has thus been justifiably read in consonance with the Song of Songs: "Let him kiss me with the kisses of his mouth."[2]

The Pact of Sinai cannot be considered superseded in the new covenant because it is contracted even "with him also who is not here today."[3] The exclusivity of the choice must be strictly maintained, but its aim in the divine plan is that "all the tribes of the earth shall bless themselves by you,"[4] which already is clearly expressed in the pact with Abraham and reinforced by the prophets. Only by living to the fullest, to the immanent finality—the autoteleology—of its divine election, does the historical and theological Israel arrive at the universal vocation that was already present in the divine plan from the very beginning.

The "ten words" are *both spoken and written*; they are neither *only* spoken nor *only* written. There is a primacy of the oral Torah over the written Torah, because in all of holy history the Lord systematically opposes the recurrent attempt to appropriate and therefore absolutize the spoken or written word instead of listening, as he insists, to His voice.[5] There is a symmetry between God's demand that we not sequester His teaching, his invitation to maintain ourselves always in the life of our relation with Him, and the preeminence the biblical tradition accords the oral Torah over the written Torah.

In other words, because the "ten words" have been given to a people and therefore to a living entity, it is only by entering into a relationship with it—this people with its tradition, with its generational responsibility (*paradosis*)—that we will be able to have access to the vital meaning of words that are already spoken and already written. The reality of a people supposes a common lineage, and no one can take part in its patrimony without entering into the generative dynamic, binding oneself to a sort of extrapolation of its fragments (*excerpta*). The interlocutor of the "ten words" (the "you" of the Lord) is both the people understood as a unity and every single person within it. When the Lord says "You," His "I" means neither the people alone nor the individual alone. The covenant always involves the truth of each man and, at the same time, of all of mankind. The simultaneity of this personal and social involvement also dictates the historical and existential modality of the vital permanence of the "ten words" and of access to them.

The primacy of "saying" carries another important primacy—that of the first three words over the others. Using the Christian formulation: "You shall have no gods except me," "You shall not utter the name of Yahweh your God to misuse it," and "Remember the Sabbath day and keep it holy." These three words enjoy a triple prominence: (1) in them the Lord expresses Himself in the first person, (2) all subsequent words derive from and depend on them, and (3) all of the subsequent words refer back to them—that is to say, to the Subject who speaks.

It is in the relation of the covenant (I am yours/You are mine) and therefore of belonging to it that the Lord's teachings, norms, prescriptions, decrees, and commands take form.[6] The words that follow the first three, in turn, permit their effective actualization. From this point of view, "all these words"[7] are a single word. The "ten words" are given, but they never separate or free themselves from the Lord. This is what marks the distinction of the "ten words" from the numerous precepts (*mišpatim*) and norms (*mizvot*) that Moses gave to the people. Such a distinction keeps the "ten words" from being reduced to the status of precepts or rules; instead they perform the mediating function between the fundamental act of assent to the pact and the categorical act of ethical conduct. After God has acted, our relation with Him becomes a measure of morality. Our relation with God and our ethics are connected and inseparable because they rest in the recollection of what God does and in the observance of His words through which man can perceive the path of true personal and social good.

As a result, it is evident that, for the believer, the first responsibility is the decision to remain in the pact and to live within the vicinity of the Presence. That implies the conversion of the life, the mind, and the heart. It asks that the whole humanity of man be invested in it: the life of faith and moral life are equally called into play. Only once we have let ourselves be aware of the reality of the pact, in experience and in history, can the Decalogue shine forth in all its splendor.

Throughout modernity, on the other hand, two sequential divisions have occurred: first in the tablet from God's covenant and then next in the second tablet from the first. As a result there has been an inevitable reduction of the words of the second tablet to moral and legal prescriptions. Today this division has so exhausted its historical effect of secularizing and emancipating ethics that even the simply normative aspect of the Decalogue no longer carries much weight.

A similar line of development was predictable: it is very problematic to attempt to conserve a serene and binding moral conscience without recognizing that the effort must refer to a beneficent and higher authority.

After the fall of our progenitors, if we do not stay within the limits of the pact, we will not be able to recognize and respect the truth of the very order of creation. In fact, it has acquired the sense of entering into the communion of the covenant, which gives sufficient and historical reason to love and respect the order of the creature. At the beginning of the third millennium it is clear to us what the Lord himself revealed at Sinai: we cannot effectively sustain the truth of creation if we do not enter into the truth of the covenant-pact.

CHRISTIANITY AND RATIONAL, UNIVERSAL MORALS

That the "ten words" are originally and always the major criteria of religious morals does not mean that the rational, moral conscience (or the "natural" conscience that is, in a limited sense, non*revealed*) may be incapable of truth. The vicissitudes of the late Middle Ages (especially with the rediscovery of Aristotle and the work of Thomas Aquinas) and then of modernity have shown the importance of the rational, moral conscience—its autonomous ability to construct an ethical form. Theological thought, likewise, has been able to recognize that revelation does not substitute for but rather conserves moral autonomy, which, thus recognized, becomes elevated by faith as an act of the creature within a wider and more radical belonging to his God.

Better still: moral sentiments that are common, fundamental, and spontaneous must be historically interpreted as an anthropological horizon that is indispensible for being able to comprehend the original and definitive meaning of the divine "ten words." The "ten words" cannot then be reduced to rational morality: both they and moral sentiment enter into play, the former as the height of moral significance (the "ten words") and the latter as its true, anticipatory question (common moral meaning). It is not by chance that the doctrine of the Church fathers perceives, in the second tablet of the commandments, the fundamental moral contents of an upright conscience and a natural moral conscience: St. Thomas will see, in their *lex naturalis*, "participation" in eternal, divine wisdom (*lex aeterna*), that is, of the eternal Word made flesh in God.

Considered not as a pure religion but in its true nature as a universal, concrete event, Christianity unveils an ethical universality that encompasses moral law and, at the same time, transcends it—witness, for example, the Gospel's story of the rich young man.[1] Jesus, who is himself the living fulfillment of the law, is also himself a living and personal law, presenting himself through revelation as the dynamic synthesis of internal and intrinsic morals. This dynamic presents itself according to the rhythm of *promise*, *commandment*, and *love*.[2] In fact, the commandment is tied to a promise that constitutes its raison d'être. In the Old Testament, it is the promise of land for an existence of freedom and justice; in the New Testament, it is the promise of the kingdom that marks the passage from the regime of slavery to that of the children of God.[3] The two Testaments have in common the idea of the promise of the gift of true life, which consists of a renewed relation (communion-in-love) with God and with other human beings. The promise explicitly reveals itself and fulfills itself in Jesus. As such, there is no conflict between the event of Jesus of Nazareth and moral law while speaking of Jesus as a living and personal law[4]—one that transcends natural law.

Jesus in fact demonstrates what personal participation in divine life can be and how the commandments may in reality show a way to the perfection of love. Therefore Christian morals consist of the love of Christ as a motivation for observing the commandments. If we assume, as a moral rule, the action of Jesus—His word, His precepts, following Christ and clinging to the very person of Christ—we find, in communion with Him, an adequate reason for a moral sense for existence. This is why Christ is the essential and original principle of Christian morals. As for the principle of universal morals, they conserve in themselves and give value to the path of human moral experience as such, so revelation does not deny them; instead, it unveils in their contents the rhythm of promise, commitment, and love.

In fact, as moral experience is rooted in an originary relation with the good, so it is oriented toward the maturity of human perfection (love), which encompasses moral maturity and, at the same time, transcends it in the anthropological fullness of love. It opens, by its very nature, the desire not only for upright conduct but also for a condition of complete happiness.

In short, although the relation to the person of Christ confirms the universal value of rational moral law, it also reveals that this same universality cannot be entrusted to dependence on universal norms alone but is instead rewritten within a personal relation. In Christ, this "living and personal law," the universal and personal dimensions of moral life, are miraculously synthesized. Without losing its universal value—but rather confirming and deepening it—morality acquires in Christianity the consciousness that the meaning of anthropological and moral good has a privileged relation to its genesis, manifestation, and fulfillment [*attuazione*]. The centrality of the connection with the human-divine person of Jesus thus demonstrates in a unique and exemplary way the personalistic universality—or better, the universalistic personalism—of moral experience.

This, then, is the teaching of the Jewish and Christian model of revelation: the close relation between the first three commandments of the Decalogue (which focus on the honor rendered exclusively to God), and the remaining seven (which govern moral conduct), indicates, in turn, that moral law is anchored in the truth. As exclusive adoration, respect, and worship must be reserved for God because He is the only true God, so too the "moral" commandments are such not because they are commanded but because they are true. Moral truth means that the commandment is not in and of itself limit and restriction, even if it is a negative sign, but instead that it points to something universally and always worth avoiding, so that truth may fall in line with action and may blossom within our own life and the lives of others.

In other words, the rootedness of the commandment in divine truth proclaims that the foundation of moral experience lies in an originary belonging. The rational moral conscience says that its imperatives have a great deal to do with a common anthropological belonging, one in which every moral agent is involved.

These two characteristics are critical to the quality of the contents of the moral precepts according to the Decalogue. They indicate that the value of every norm, according to its specific contents, is to safeguard and promote the truth of the community [*appartenenza*] in which the moral agent himself is included. We understand then that harming another is prohibited, in so far as that other is "part" of ourselves [*"parte" di sé*] and in ourselves in relation with others. Thus he who kills in some way murders himself—to the precise degree that, along with the other he destroys, he also destroys the ontological bonds with the other human and with God, bonds that are so essential to him.

YOU SHALL NOT KILL

"You shall not kill" is the commandment in the Decalogue that expresses the inviolable value of human beings' lives in the eyes of God. From the standpoint of
the rational moral conscience and of philosophical
thought, to what does this correspond? What part of God's
vision of man is visible even to human reason?

God sees his image in man. Philosophical reason,
meanwhile, is able to see in man an exceptional gift—his
capacity to open himself up to the entire horizon of reality, with his interest and questioning, his intuition and
reasoning, his desire and affection—that positions him
as a singular being in the universe. From all this, man
derives his ability to interpret and transform reality, to
produce forms and culture, to construct and live in the
world. This, in turn, renders man both different from all
other living creatures and involved with all beings. Man

is the being who establishes relations in all directions because he is himself an ego-in-relation [*io-in-relazione*] and is capable of placing himself in thought and action in relation with all fellow beings and, moreover, with all of reality.

Reasoning of this sort puts man in the center of the world because the "world" (which is more than just a quantifiable cosmos) exists only by reason of its center. There is no coherence to the repeated attempts to cast man as merely one creature among many (perhaps a bit superior, yes, but without the irreducible originality it would take to embrace all of reality with his talents and, as such, to "create the world"). Whoever theorizes the partial quality of man (his being as nothing but a mere piece of the cosmos) always, of course, posits that quality in relation to a totality of referents that, in turn, is seen precisely through man's thought: man is construed as part of the whole thought by the very person who thinks man only as one part of the whole (physical aggregation, biological organism, psychic apparatus, social function, etc.). Whoever reduces man to a mere part, in other words, inevitably does so in reference to a certain totality of the world: physical cosmos, biological world, evolution, whole social fabric, etc. One can then conceive man as a "part" only insofar as one contradicts oneself pragmatically, claiming the very opposite of what one does. Human thought that speaks of man as just a part does so precisely by theorizing the whole of which man is part. The reductionism that pretends to define human existence with reference to partial categories is founded—and invalidates itself—in this contradiction.

This sort of human capacity is a manifestation of something invisible yet powerful. We can give it any of the many names that historical Western thought has used: thought, subjectivity, transcendentality, soul—none of them equivalent, of course, but all converging on the idea of a constitutive nucleus of human identity in which the human is understood to be essential, unsurpassable, unfathomable. It cannot be undone except through the most difficult operation of radical, materialistic reductionism—which, however, leaves us with no plausible explanation for the unequivocal differences that operate in the cultures of man.

This glory of being, which is man, is the place where the vision of God meets human thought itself. And precisely this is the proper object of the prohibition "You shall not kill."

(a) *Why should we not kill?* The theological conscience answers this way: because man is created "in the image and likeness of God," and the killing of man, who is the object of God's satisfaction,[1] marks an affront and disdain toward God. Here, by contrast, is the response of the philosophical tradition that has lent its vocabulary to the modern-contemporary culture of liberty and human rights: we should not kill because, as Kant argues, man is the bearer of "an unconditioned, incomparable worth" beyond price.[2]

But the reason of "You shall not kill" requires a deeper examination, one decisive in regard to any appreciation of the radical nature of the prohibition and of the meaning of the norm.

What one should not want to kill is man considered in his own anthropological identity—or, to be more exact, his transcendental nature. He has a dignity beyond price because it is incomparable and, as such, is the condition of every experience, action, relation, meaning. As we have said, it is the condition of appearance of the world, which is to say, of the intentional and cultural relation through which man opens up the world around himself—in other words, reality inasmuch as it is conceived, interpreted, and transformed. Transcendentality means thought, desire, will, freedom; it is therefore the condition for the encounter among men as well for their intersubjective and socializing relations.

Examining the commandment more carefully means affirming that, as we have noted before, to want to kill the whole anthropological being is not possible without contradiction, in a twofold sense. In the first place, because killing construes transcendental human identity as something that can be exchanged, bartered with another, or sacrificed for another. In fact, he who kills is motivated by evasion of harm for himself or others (and through others again for himself). He does it to avenge something for himself or others, to exact payment for a material or moral debt owed to him or others, to sacrifice others for a higher good, to render others as tribute to a Master-God . . . In every case, dignity is equiparated with something inferior to it or made the object of something superior to it. In every case, dignity is reduced to an object: the very source of all possible experience becomes an object measured against and subordinated to a particular feeling—anger, cupidity, or revenge—or it is rendered the object of anonymous interest for a historical project (the Third Reich, world communism, technocratic globalization) or of some God so impotent that he needs his creature's blood, etc. The violence of killing consists essentially in this disparity of levels through which one human is objectified and the other reduced to a thing—an objectification, we note, that is really only imagined or willed because it is impossible in reality: if man were objectifiable, he simply would not be the subjective, transcendental being that he is.

The second sense of the contradictory nature of the act of killing is involved in the first. As we have stated, it is the homicidal will that's violent because it is vain if it claims to reduce the priceless dignity of man to an exchangeable thing (your entire humanity for my wrong or for the satisfaction of a God). In turn, the irrational vanity of killing is such because it looks for something ultimately impossible: at its most radical, it claims to kill what, by its very nature, cannot be killed. We always have attributed to man's transcendental identity and spiritual subjectivity some form of survival: they are evident both in his bond and in his transcendence with respect to the space and time of the physical, the biological, and the social (if it were not so, in fact, there simply would be no symbolic order and cultural patrimony). Homicidal hatred, which is capable of the harm of killing the historic exercise of subjectivity, is, however, powerless to destroy man's intimate, secret, and ineffable core.

Killing is not as powerful [*potente*] as is believed, as Christ has also said: "Do not be afraid of those who kill the body but cannot kill the soul; fear him rather who can destroy both body and soul in hell."[3] Man can end up, however, in a condition in which his whole being is reduced to a state that is completely in contradiction with his nature and his vocation. Man cannot die. But he can end up in a dead life; he can become the living dead.

(b) *A deep and meaningful study.* The contradictoriness of the act of killing is at the heart of the thought of Emmanuel Lévinas.[4] His identification of the face of the other with the commandment "You shall not kill" is an emblematic way of posing the question of indispensability of every human identity.[5] But it is also a equivocal mode that easily becomes a naive sentimentalism if one does not explicate the theological pivot on which it rests. Lévinas's point of departure is the fact that the face is the sign of the inviolable independence of the other man: No one can truly possess someone who cannot be completely reduced to a disposable thing. Precisely this inviolability, however, gives rise to the temptation of homicide: if I cannot possess you, I destroy you. This is why, as Lévinas affirms, "I can wish to kill only an existent absolutely independent, which exceeds my powers infinitely, and therefore does not oppose them but paralyzes the very power of power."[6]

Lévinas's provocation refers to the facility with which we can push the other to the outside, most of all when he is effectively helpless. What this means is that the face of the other is inviolable not because I am unable to entirely exclude the other but because the face of the other embodies a transcendence. The face of the other thus "opposes to me not a greater force, an energy assessable and consequently presenting itself as though it were part of a whole, but the very transcendence of his being by relation to the whole; not some superlative of power, but precisely the infinity of his transcendence."[7]

This explains the thesis of "infinite resistance to murder." Lévinas formalizes this with the commandment "You shall not commit murder,"[8] which he sees inscribed on or, better, identified with the face of the other: "The infinite paralyzes power by its infinite resistance to murder, which, firm and insurmountable, gleams in the face of the Other, in the total nudity of his defenseless eyes, in the nudity of the absolute openness of the Transcendent."[9] "To see a face," Lévinas says elsewhere, "is already to hear 'You shall not kill.' "[10] The sense of Lévinas's reasoning is that "the impossibility of killing is not real, but moral."[11] Homicide is obviously possible, but only "when one has not looked at the Other in the face," which is precisely also when the first word ("You shall not kill") has not been understood. If instead "the uncrossable infinite" of face is gazed upon and understood, "all murderous intent is immersed and submerged."[12]

This conclusion has an interesting anthropological corollary: although the violent man is sovereign (since he effectively has power), he is also alone (since he does not step outside himself, since he recognizes no one beyond himself), such that seeing and understanding a face means being together. Lévinas asserts that "the commerce with beings . . . begins with 'You shall not kill.'"[13] He claims that whoever is touched by this word also touches the inalienable transcendence of the other, which is the requirement for every social bond worthy of humanity.

Lévinas's entire reasoning is governed by a divine reference that today is very easy to put between parentheses. In Lévinas, however, we are always dealing with an inescapable reference: The voice that makes itself understood in the face ("You shall not kill") is the very voice of God himself ("everything I can hear [*entendre*] coming from God or going to God, Who is invisible, must have come to me via the one, unique voice").[14] This means that it is not possible to separate the insuperable infinity inscribed on the "speaking" face of the other from the infinity of the God who shines through it and, as such, lets himself be understood. Or, in short: the ultimate reason the other cannot be killed is that his creaturely alterity partakes in the creative alterity of God.

To prove this inescapable theological foundation, it is worth noting that Lévinas reads the commandment "You shall not kill" as an extension of "I am Yahweh your God,"[15] in conformity with a midrash that dictates that the "ten words" must be set up in two columns so that the first word fits together, precisely, with the sixth.[16]

(c) *The primary meaning of not killing.* This ontological and anthropological investigation helps us understand the primary meaning of "You shall not kill." It warns man to avoid (philosophically) irrational and (theologically) blasphemous conduct because that conduct is inhabited by a radical contradiction in relation to the meaning and possibility of destroying the life of man (either of another or oneself, homicide or suicide). It clearly seems that ethical autonomy can never involve a normative subjectivism. Autonomy means being able to give an account to oneself of inconsistency of one's action and, at the same time, indicates a person's capacity to establish the moral prohibition that saves man from a tragic contradiction: the simultaneous destruction of the world of the victim's concrete possibilities and the meaningfulness of the executioner's own action, the historical existence of one and the moral dignity of the other.

If this is the justification of the prohibition, it seems that a materialist culture (as updated with whatever form of reductionism, whether physicalist, economic, functionalist, etc.) can justify the prohibition of homicide in various ways, but always in a mode necessarily extrinsic in relation to anthropological identity as such. It will sustain the individual and collective instinct of self-defense, prevent social harm, preserve the collective good, safeguard public order, etc. But never will it be able to provide a reason having to do with an anthropological nature endowed with characteristics that are irreducible because structurally inalienable. A fortiori there will be no arguments nullifying the moral prohibition against suicide. In fact, the major social experiments of twentieth-century materialism (Nazism and communism), like the more barbarous forms of capitalism and colonialism, have demonstrated that a certain regulation of homicidal violence is always necessary to maintain a society. But they also demonstrate that, in the absence of a consistent humanism, the spaces for such violence also widen at a worrisome rate, especially in the form of sacrifice of human life on the altar of "superior" interests.

To this one might respond (and some usually do) that even in personalist, Christian humanism the idea of legitimate defense prevails. In addition, one would have to add the subject of just war, the use of public force, up to the armed conflict that suppresses crime, etc., all of which tend to assimilate the same criteria in their reasoning, whether in individual or social form.

Homicide differs from these uses of force, which do reach the level of killing human lives, not because of the different values placed on the human lives in play but because the use of lethal force is here in the role of defense.

Homicide entails an asymmetry with the use of force on the part of the aggressor. For him, the use of force is an exercise of violence because it is an aggressive force based on a systematic, self-justifying principle, with a kind of subjective, irrevocable legitimization. What legitimizes defense is precisely its intrinsic limitation: defense renounces, on principle, the supposed "right" to the use of aggressive force, using force solely to avoid harm to the innocent.

(d) *The indispensability of life.* The other face of materialism is *spiritualism.* However obsolete this term may seem, it is nevertheless still useful to link together a number of contemporary positions culled from the trend to protect the free exercise of subjectivity apart from its tie with prevoluntary biological and psychosomatic reality. This position is evident in more than a few cult followers of bioethics and biopolitics—for example, in the infelicitously framed debate between the sanctity and quality of life or in gender theory's claim about the separation of gender identity and biological sexuality.

The distinction and opposition between the sanctity of life and the quality of life seems to suggest a concept of human life bifurcated between the biological and biographical, the objective and subjective, between what is given and what is experienced, what is lived and what is constructed.

The concept of "quality of life," which today takes the place of the concept of sanctity, has been understood as a collection of parameters that allow us to establish the real worth of every human life. Having lost all ontological referents, the dignity of "persons" would seem to be defined here by a combination of anthropological data (in particular, operative capacities) that in principle can undergo quite extreme changes. So, for example, if the person can be defined on the basis of the selective criteria of self-awareness, rationality, and moral sense (possibilities of being praised or blamed), qualities of life that render life worthy of being lived, then life will be bound to those parameters—which, however, are not possessed by all human beings in all conditions. This, in turn, allows us to remove from some human beings the quality of the person. Understood in these comparative, historical, and variable terms, the concept of "dignity" generates a distinction between the simply human life and the worthy human life—the life of the *person*—and offers parameters for the legitimate, direct, and intentional destruction of a human life.

But, as Theodor W. Adorno and Max Horkheimer observe, life that is placed entirely back into the hands of man comes to be considered fully comprehensible by its categories, rendered completely equivalent to preselected criteria, with the result that it is entirely "objectified" and disposable.[17] As in the strictest physicalist reductionism, attempts to attribute value and quality to life that do not refer back to any subjectivity transcending the empirical and cultural leaves life totally comprehensible and also totally disposable.

(e) *The sphere of biopolitics.* The sphere of biopolitics, therefore, becomes a treacherous terrain, one on which there is a tendency to dismantle the theory of the indispensability of human life. The ideas that prevail today assume the very opposite of life's inviolability, supposing instead that life progressively has become an object of minute control by power, to the point where power itself now decides when a life is worthy of living and when it deserves to end. Michel Foucault has noted the epochal transition: whereas in the past, the old concept of sovereign power assumed as its object the capacity "to kill or let live," today the situation seems reversed, so that, for contemporary biopower, we now deal with the power "to make live and let die."[18] Or, as Giorgio Agamben expresses it, we deal with the power to "make survive" as authorized by an ambiguous concept of "care of life" that, in turn, tends toward a progressive state regulation of the biological, about which many intellectuals (for example, Jürgen Habermas) have expressed concern.

Equally worrisome is the fact that, when life enters the horizon of political disposability, power's decisions have inevitable effects not only on individuals but also on the whole fate of the human species.[19]

Most worrisome of all is the fact that this more or less total political disposability of life elicits no moral rebellion. It is instead reinforced by a united and widespread approval. Biopower can claim a more or less generalized consensus because it presents itself with a beneficent face, which in turn rests on a symptomatic separation: on the one hand, we have worthy human life (constituted by relations with the world and with others, so that life possesses a standard "quality" irrefutable for all), whereas on the other hand we have biological life (consisting of nothing more than the subsistence of our animal organism).

Now, "normally" it is self-evident that we are the masters of these "two" lives. But when it happens that these two lives somehow diverge—an event that is easily possible today, such as when an individual loses certain qualitative standards that claim to "certify" human life's dignity—we run into the problem of who then becomes the administrator of the residual organic life, of the remnants of the organic life that in some way remain even in the absence of its legitimate and natural proprietor. At this point the "beneficent" power intervenes, advancing the thesis (by now widespread) that the destruction of a human life that has been "reduced" to a mere biological function is not only *not* homicide but in fact is the best way to take care of that life. With this, the destruction of life thus becomes an accomplishment of civilization, which manages to advance despite the barbarisms of a morality that still insists on defending the taboo of the sanctity of life. This, precisely, is the rhetoric of the famous "Plea for Beneficent Euthanasia" of 1974.[20]

RESPONSIBILITIES AND CHALLENGES: BURNING ISSUES

It is clear that, for whoever lives within the Judeo-Christian tradition, the first responsibility that issues from the commandment "You shall not kill" consists of deciding to remain within the covenant-pact and thence too of advocating that all men follow the dictates of rational, universal moral law. This responsibility is never obvious; it ever renews itself, and indeed its perennial renewal is an inexhaustible source of wonder and joy. The covenant-pact and the rational recognition of the splendor of the truth of fundamental moral experience, which shines in every man, is not a thing of the past. It is the primary source for trustworthy hope for the future.[1]

That involves a permanent conversion of life, mind, and heart, which requires an interweaving of good relations and virtuous practice. Not by chance does the Bible assert that the yoke of the Torah is not borne alone.

The book of the prophet Zephaniah speaks of serving the Lord "under the same yoke,"[2] "with one shoulder," that is, shoulder to shoulder. This is how the Decalogue, especially "You shall not kill," will be able to shine forth in its full brilliance.

Recently there has been a great deal of research and discussion about the fifth commandment. As we have seen, "You shall not kill" weaves the biblical world together with the realms of the philosophical, theological, juridical, anthropological, etc., obliging us to answer two central questions that address the meaning and object of the commandment. First, *what does it mean to kill?* And, second, *whom should I not kill?*

These two questions, in turn, uncover solid ground for the exploration of two other questions—two of the most burning questions that can be posed in the current public debate in relation to life (especially its origin) and death.

(a) *What, in truth, is life?* In the first place, the issue of the object of the commandment poses to us an epistemological problem, one in which biology, philosophy, and theology meet: "What, in truth, is life?"[3] Spaemann claims: "One speaks of human rights in the absolute, and yet one is not authorized to define the characteristics that should be possessed by the bearers of these rights."[4] In fact, when these rights (understood in their deepest meaning) lose their breadth and rootedness, the very concept of rights and the foundation of democracy fall apart too. Spaemann points out to us the grave danger that is harbored in a certain way of laying out the question about the nature of life: "Who can be legitimately considered a person?"[5] But, as the encyclical *Evangelium Vitae* asks, taking up a passage from *Donum Vitae* (I.1), "How could a human individual not be a human person?"[6]

We must pose a similar question, above all, about life's beginning and end. Departing from a debatable interpretation of the Aristotelian and Thomasian theories of reproduction, some, like Norman Ford, maintain that the human embryo is not yet a separate individual (and therefore hardly a person) until after the fourteenth day after conception, since before that moment it can still divide itself into more individuals.[7] We can object by clarifying that, in the Aristotelian view, the embryo is already a human being *in potentia* and therefore able, by virtue of its own power, to become a human being *in actus*, so long as no obstacles are put in its way. Its soul is intellective even if, until its organs develop, the embryo exercises only its sensory and nutritive faculties.[8]

Ford's theory and the theories of those like him represent partial and even, in some ways, diminished obedience to "You shall not kill." The greater challenge springs from so-called scientific neutrality. Some say that, to determine what is life and who is a person, biology should remain ethically neutral.[9] With Hans Jonas we may disassemble this supposed neutrality, judging it not only undesirable but also impossible. Its pragmatic contradiction has been documented by three scientists

(Ernest Brücke, Emil Du Bois-Reymond, and Herman Helmholtz), who promised to pursue in their research the theory that an organism reacts only to physical-chemical forces. This eluded them, Jonas observed, because the very fact of their having made a promise ended up making it impossible for them to make good on the specific content of the promise itself. In the event, the scientists were bound less by the principle of keeping their minds open to future discoveries than by their initial preconception—their promise.[10]

Here we see the return of the concept of "quality of life," which in this instance comes to be understood as a confluence of measurable criteria that would allow us to establish the real worth of every human life. The dignity of the person could be defined with the aid of different data that might change over the course of a human being's life. Thus not all human beings would be persons because not all are capable of self-awareness, rationality, or moral sense (possibility of being praised or blamed).[11]

As we have seen, we must then distinguish between two types of life: one purely biological and the other biographical.[12] Between these two, as Bernard Baertschi maintains, we must search for a balance of values, calculating the various qualities that make life the object of interest.[13] This comparative and ever-variable method therefore distinguishes between simply human life and a worthy human life (the only one fitting for a person). When the quality of life is too low, the direct, intentional destruction of human life is permissible.

Peter Singer's position on this issue is the most extreme. For Singer, the interest, value, and therefore the rights of a human individual would depend on his rationality and self-consciousness, understood as the capacity to experience pleasure, feel pain, and understand their value.[14]

In the case of abortion, for example, a fiction that a human being is not involved would be maintained (the "pro-choice" position). According to Singer, many supporters of abortion look for empty compromise on this question. He asserts instead that it would be more correct to recognize that "thousands of years of lip-service to the Christian ethic have not succeeded in suppressing entirely the earlier ethical attitude that newborn-infants, especially if unwanted, are not yet full members of the moral community."[15] On these terms, when the life of a child would be so painful as to be not worth living, and in the absence of any external reasons to keep the baby alive (such as the feelings of the parents, that is, their pleasure or pain), then it would be better to kill him. Analogously, we should act the same in the case of a terminally ill patient, when there is biological life but the biographical life has ceased: The body is alive, but the person is no longer there.[16]

One variant of Singer's thought is formulated in a manual on bioethics edited by several Oxford scholars.[17] The biological humanist vision, which does not consider the difference between the human being in a biological sense (belonging to the human species) and in a moral sense (accepted members of the community), is overcome by means of the category of self-interest. Human embryos do not have self-interest (because they are not sentient); ergo they do not have "moral status," and we owe them only the respect we give to "moral values" such as a dead body or the flag of one's country.

The extremism of Singer's proposal and its diffusion confirm, in the most disturbing way, the harsh and even excessive diagnosis made by Adorno and Horkheimer about the results of the Enlightenment and the tendencies of contemporary culture: "Myth is already enlightenment, and enlightenment reverts back to mythology."[18] Thus "each of the Ten Commandments is declared void before the tribunal of formal reason. They are revealed without exception as ideologies."[19] In the Marquis de Sade's *Juliette*, "the Pope himself pleads the case for murder. He finds it easier to rationalize un-Christian acts in the light of natural reason than it had ever been to justify the Christian principles according to which those acts were devilish. The 'mitered philosopher' has less need of sophistry in advocating murder than Maimonides and St. Thomas Aquinas in condemning it."[20]

The aggravation of subjectivism, which courses through modernity as a temptation, is paradoxically destined to favor the supremacy of the coldest naturalistic objectivism. Life reduced to the experience of pleasure and pain ends up promoting a vitalism of functions and capacities as the criterion of worth.

(b) *To control one's own death?* The change in the way of thinking about life also reveals itself in the growing desire, always spreading among the citizens of modern democracies, to control the modalities of one's own death.[21] With this focus we are obliged to confront problems of suicide and euthanasia within Catholic theology, even while studies in the medical, juridical, and theological spheres also proliferate.[22]

The Kantian foundation of the dignity of the person (his distinction between dignity and price, between intrinsic good and something for which some sort of equivalent could be substituted) leads us to consider this dignity as a moral end that always is to be respected. All the same, some critics maintain that Kant, by positing a priori the foundation of dignity in the possibility of self-reference, in the autonomy of the will, in one's own self-consciousness,[23] actually ends up limiting dignity to a *faktum* of mere consciousness that is ultimately very fragile.[24] Kantians, however, reject this critique of Kant, asserting that the philosopher's concept of autonomy does not correspond to the concepts of self-reference and self-awareness but deals instead with the transcendental "objectivity" of human subjectivity.

The force of the precept "You shall not kill," understood in relation to the burning issues of the beginning and end of life, must be sought in another direction. Above all, we must return to Lévinas's proposal: the meaning of human life emerges in the encounter with the other and, specifically, with his face. "The relation to the face is immediately ethical. The face is what one cannot kill, or at least it is that whose meaning consists in saying:

'thou shalt not kill.'"[25] This is, for Lévinas, the first and central commandment, the one that underlies the others and inaugurates the human act of responsibility.

The irreducibility of every human individual to *something* is unveiled in his face. In this sense, as Spaemann has shown, persons are given to one another not as objects *about whom* one speaks or *of whom* one disposes but instead as subjects *with whom* to speak and *to whom* to give respect.[26] This acceptance of the person as someone—which is the most fundamental basis of every other further duty—permits us to avoid reducing life to one measurable factor among so many others and to reevaluate the worth of the gift that every human life reveals. Responsibility in the face of life is then precisely not an object of choice; it is assumed in a moment of freedom anterior to any choice: before decision or spontaneity, there is the acceptance of the person (gift). In this same way, the dignity of the person is a given: it is not based on a reflective moment of self-awareness or on a judgment of reason about itself.[27] This has been demonstrated by Gabriel Marcel, who used the image of the marriage contract to describe the relation between man and his life: "It seems as though it were necessary to postulate the existence of a pact, I should almost say a nuptial bond, between man and life; it is in man's power to untie this bond, but insofar as he denies the pact he tends to lose the notion of his existence."[28]

Taking Marcel's insight as his point of departure and carefully reading the current cultural climate, the theologian Giuseppe Angelini proposes to consider life not as a specific chapter in human ethics but as the principle of all ethics. From this perspective, to understand "you shall not kill," we cannot look for a material and objective definition of what life may be apart from the relation of one man with another—that is, with the *I-in-relation* [*io-in-relazione*]. Killing as an act here gets reimagined from the standpoint of possible human freedom and intention in relationship to the other. But if the life of the other is not only a physical reality to be respected but also an intention, an expectation, and an appeal, then killing is always excommunication—exclusion from communication.[29]

From the perspective of a morality of the first person, the intrinsic, intentional character of action is essential in understanding moral values. *What is it to kill?* Killing confronts us not with a simple, physical act but with a direct and voluntary action. It is not simply an event that just happens; it is an act willed by someone. The relation between an action that is, at base, intentional and the ultimate aims that motivate that action permits us to understand the meaning of killing: it is an intrinsically evil act that admits no exceptions. That same relation also explains the sense in which legitimate defense, and the eventual pain of death inflicted with justice, may not be exceptions, even though they do not really count in the case of the commandment we are considering.[30]

From this point of view, the moral act of suicide must be considered in a relation of reciprocity with murder.

Suicide, in essence, is the murder of "myself as another," whereas murder is "suicide of myself in another" (or at least the practical predisposition toward suicide).[31] And euthanasia, which takes its place between the desire for death and the flight from death,[32] demands a rethinking of the event of death focused on an abandonment of meaning achieved in life itself.[33]

Consideration of the ever-intentional character of the gaze at the other does not therefore simply require that "You shall not kill" and that you shall respect life. Rather, from a relational perspective, the commandment is revealed as a call to the acceptance and recognition of the other that can never be severed from a quest to further his success. For this reason, Benedict XVI strongly proposes a definition of the human person that is centered on being in relation.[34] To promote life therefore involves a commitment in the first person, within all spheres of human existence, to enhance the good relations that are constitutive of the "I" from its very inception.

This is the most fecund content, on both a personal and social level, of a commandment that always—but today, perhaps, with fresh urgency—enjoins us: "you shall not kill."

PART II

The Archaeology of Homicide

ADRIANA CAVARERO

A SPECIAL LAW

"The entire Torah, in its minute descriptions, is concentrated in the 'Thou Shalt not kill' that the face of the other signifies,"[1] writes the Jewish philosopher Emmanuel Lévinas. Aside from finding a confirmation in Jewish doctrine, this sentence sums up Lévinas's thought as a whole—a radical ethic of nonviolence that, reached through the author's anomalous reading of the sixth commandment, can serve as an introduction to our theme here. We begin with Lévinas because we believe in the rhetorical efficacy of contrasts. And, in this case, the contrast is considerable. Against almost all tradition, Lévinas reads the commandment as an absolute prohibition against homicide that contemplates no exceptions. For him, "You shall not kill" is an unconditional principle that holds forever and in every circumstance. It is in force in time of war, it excludes capital punishment, and it does not even justify legitimate defense.

Stated in a brief formula, and paraphrasing Lévinas's interpretation, we therefore could say that the word of God in the Decalogue enjoins us *never* to kill. Contradicted by millennia of history and doctrines, this thesis is simple—and seems completely absurd. Indeed, today as in the past, the reigning conviction is the opposite: under certain circumstances, killing is just and necessary.

Examined with philosophic curiosity, "You shall not kill" reveals itself to have a special status with respect to all of the other commandments in the Decalogue. Even though this commandment might claim the "*always*" and the "*never*" more than any other commandment, it nevertheless does not bear out these adverbs: it does not give support for the notion that "You shall not kill" should be substantially understood as an absolute, unconditional, radical prohibition against homicide. "*Always* honor your father and mother" and "*Never* steal" sound, to our ears, to be sentences that are enriched by the adverb, not modified by them. "*Never* kill," on the other hand, not only profoundly changes that assumption but also contradicts millennia of history. Cases in which killing a man is permitted and just abound not only in the Bible but also in the dominant traditions of Jewish and Christian treatises.[2] The same goes for modern political and juridical culture, where killing is permitted for legitimate defense, to punish murder, and, above all, in war. The paradox is already announced in a passage in Genesis 9.6 in which God declares: "I will demand an account of your life-blood . . . I will demand an account of every man's life from his fellow men." After this verse, God proclaims: "He who sheds man's blood, / shall have his blood shed by man, / for in the image of God / man was made." Here, the very same criterion—being made in the image of God—prohibits homicide and also dictates the killing of the killer. Does the killer thus lose his essence as a man? Or could it be that he has lost that resemblance to God which characterizes the very humanity of man? This question, far from appearing absurd, traditionally implies a positive response. We will sum it up here in the words of John Locke's *Second Treatise of Government*, written at the end of the seventeenth century and given as a commentary on Genesis: Whoever has spilled human blood "therefore may be destroyed as a lion or a tiger."[3] That an analogous zoological declassification could be applied in the sphere of war seems, however, somewhat problematic. Beyond the various metaphors of the feral nature of the warrior, war itself is in fact a domain that obeys the homicidal foundation of its own order: in war, the already improbable *never* of homicide changes into its exact opposite. Beginning with the very earliest narratives, "You shall not kill" falls silent on the field of battle. The rule here instead says: *always* kill the enemy.

A further—and apparently opposed—consideration confirms the special status of the sixth commandment while also highlighting the aporia in relation to the addition of "*never.*" In our times, it is amply illustrated in the thesis, espoused especially by the culture of Roman Catholicism, that the destruction of frozen embryos constitutes homicide. This thesis suggests that *never* killing a human being means not killing even the few embryonic cells that, closed up in a freezer, are also closed off from the eventual process that could bring them into being. Since there is no need to unfreeze them, and since the technology of freezing moreover can allow the embryo to last forever, the absolute prohibition against homicide in this case develops strange paradoxes. Here the commandment claims to apply itself to a most anomalous "creature"—a daughter, paradoxically, of technics. Potentially a human being, the frozen embryo is also— already on the terms of current science, to say nothing of the science to come—potentially immortal, effectively eternal as long as it is maintained in its unchanged form. Inevitable questions therefore arise. What does it mean to kill, to give death to, this creature that, unlike man, escapes the very condition of mortality? What does it mean *never* to kill something that, without ever resolving itself in the birth of anyone, can *never* "die" and in fact can *always* "live"? What concept of the human is invoked in the cause of this post-technological horizon in which the exceptional rigor of principle marries itself to its own maximum abstraction? The whole framework is marked by a kind of excess, by a desire to apply the commandment in its absolute and irrefutable form—*never* kill a man. However, this case obliges us to push the commandment still further. Instead of making the object of the prohibition an individual, living person—like the first victim Abel, a man of flesh and bone, born of a woman—the object is in fact life. Life in and of itself.

BRIEF PHILOLOGICAL NOTE

We have claimed here that "You shall not kill" is the sixth commandment, but the numbering of the commandments is notoriously controversial. Jewish tradition follows rabbinical teaching on the subdivision of the Decalogue (the *deka-logoi*, the *Ten Words*, *Aserat ha-Dibrot*) and privileges its formulation in Exodus (20.13), where "You shall not kill" comes as the sixth Word. Looking instead at the version in Deuteronomy (5.17), in conformity with the catechism of Luther (1529) and the Council of Trent (1564), Christian tradition customarily relegates the prohibition against homicide to the fifth position. In the Gospels, meanwhile, Jesus reviews the commandments several more times.[1] Even so, the most interesting philological feature is not the numbering of the commandment but rather the linguistic form it assumes in the various traditions.

Closely following the Latin "*non occides*," the Italian version of the Jerusalem Bible dictates "*non uccidere*." In the original Hebrew, by contrast, we find the verb *lirzoch* (literally "to cut into pieces"), whose meaning alludes to murder rather than to simple killing. We can say the same for the verb *phoneuō*, which appears in the Greek translation of the Septuagint and which reveals a symptomatic resonance with the term *phoinos*, which means "blood-red." The seventeenth-century King James Bible carries forward "Thou shalt not kill," but this is corrected in the updated twentieth-century edition as "You shall not murder." The distinction is hardly unimportant: "to kill" and "to murder" obviously cover different semantic territories. Within the term "murder" is already inscribed the sense of a crime, an action that provokes outrage. The meaning of "killing," on the other hand, is less fraught with the connotation of loathing and, above all, is more malleable. For example, you can kill someone by mistake, as in a hunting accident; you also could kill professionally, as do executioners or members of the military in war. But although every murder always consists of the death of a man, not every killing of a man is synonymous with murder. Of this, precisely, language assures us; the same is suggested by the various doctrines that have speculated about the sixth commandment throughout history. All of this makes the ambiguity of the verb "to kill" a source of debate.

CRIME AND PUNISHMENT

In April 2010 the D'Orsay Museum in Paris opened an exhibition that drew thousands of visitors. They were attracted first of all by its irresistibly fascinating title: "Crime and Punishment." The reference to Dostoyevsky's masterpiece is explicit. In the minds of the show's curators, crime is synonymous with murder: its paintings, photographs, illustrations, and other forms of documentation all display, in various modes, the crime of murder— that is, the individual offense. As for punishment, it is largely understood in juridical terms. Its symbol is the guillotine: the "merciful" machine, created by the French Revolution to kill in an egalitarian mode and in use in France until the abolition of capital punishment in 1981. The guillotine, in fact, welcomes visitors to the exhibition, introducing them to the artistic works that portray various ways in which constituted power [*il potere costituito*] legally kills criminals.[1] The State kills murderers—or, rather, it executes them. The commandment "You shall not kill" holds for individuals, evidently, but not for the State. The exhibition keeps silent about the common, organized method of killing en masse and on a large scale—war. Jean Clair, the creator of the exposition, has claimed that war does not immediately fit within the framework of crime and punishment. Or, more to the point, war enters into it only under rubrics marked by sharp ideological controversies that it's prudent to avoid and that pose difficult questions: Is war always a crime, or are there just wars? When can war be defined as uncontrollable murder and when a rightful punishment? It's obvious that one small show can't shoulder the burden of answering queries of such import. The visitor, however, feels pressed to pose them for himself in front of one of the first pictures in the exhibition and, finding no follow-up on his expectations, remains somewhat perplexed. On the wall of the entrance, there hangs a painting by Georg Grosz titled *Cain, or, Hitler in Hell* (1944), which depicts Hitler seated on a mountain of skeletons while the murderer of Abel lies stretched out on the ground, flat on his stomach. Both have violated the commandment "You shall not kill": this evil, which appeared with Cain, has in Hitler its final and atrocious effect. They will meet again in hell (Hitler is still alive in 1944). Inexorable, divine punishment waits for anyone who stains himself as a murderer. The proposition is clear, but it does not keep the discerning visitor from posing further and inevitable questions.

Given that we know that Hitler is one of the worst criminals in history, and given that many Western countries have by now abolished the death penalty, does the sixth commandment apply only in cases of murder? If we define murder as the killing of one innocent person, is it then permissible to kill whoever may not be innocent? But aren't most of the victims slaughtered in war precisely—innocent? What's so special about war such that it doesn't fall under the category of murder, even though in it death is dealt out en masse and, at this point, almost exclusively to civilians?

Already in its formulation within the biblical context and still in the vicissitudes of its later reception, the commandment "You shall not kill" covers a restricted area. From the beginning of human history, a vast open space contemplates multiple homicides without ever calling it by that name. "Murder, which in the case of an individual is admitted to be a crime, is called a virtue when it is committed wholesale," writes Bishop Cyprian,[2] giving voice to the radical pacifism that fed some currents in Christianity in its early centuries, only to wane from Augustine on. To be concise and move the argument along, and benefiting from Cyprian's vocabulary, we will subsume under the generic rubric "war" all those political concerns that transform homicide into virtue. In truth, even if we limit ourselves only to the twentieth century, the vocabulary of intraspecies slaughter remains very rich, articulating itself in a noteworthy series of keywords: extermination, genocide, ethnic cleansing, carnage, massacre, and more. All in all, estimates reach more than two hundred million in the century of the two World Wars. The third millennium, with its specialization in the unilateral slaughter of the helpless, has shown up to now no greater hesitation in systematically violating the principle epitomized in the sixth commandment. If, as tradition maintains in many ways, "You shall not kill" really means "You shall not kill an innocent," then vulnerable and civilian victims obviously come back into the picture. It is so much more true today that if the West wants to reflect on the meaning of "You shall not kill" it cannot proceed in terms of pure speculation outside of history. Adorno has maintained that, after Auschwitz, it is no longer possible to write poetry.[3] Nor, in truth, is it possible to think about homicide according to the constellation of meanings we've habitually used to designate this concept. Auschwitz removes the very act of killing from its traditional frames of meaning, moving beyond the distinctions between the spheres of the moral, the political, and the juridical. In fact, what meaning of "You shall not kill" remains when human violence falls on men reduced to superfluous beings whose "murder is as impersonal as the squashing of a gnat"?[4] Are we still dealing here with a scene where, in various settings, man kills man? Or have we not gone above and beyond that? The trace of this "beyond," needless to say, is still with us, even if today it takes different forms. With intermittent intensity it keeps coming back, everywhere reaffirming the "horroristic"[5] figure of our epoch: in New York, in the spectacular collapse of the Twin Towers, which claimed random victims and didn't even leave behind a cadaver; in Afghanistan and Iraq, in the heaps of entirely indistinguishable flesh of "collateral victims" struck down by drones automatically piloted from Nevada; earlier, in the 1980s, in Iran, in children transformed by Khomeini into human detonators to clear out minefields; in various places on the planet, even including London, Madrid, and Moscow, in the horrible mayhem of human bodies (at times female bodies) transformed into bombs. The various machete wars, such as those in Rwanda or Nigeria, clearly contribute to the total. Inquiries into the meaning of "You shall not kill" today, in short, must undergo a shift in perspective.

To the extent that, as Cyprian saw, war and politics always have been tied tightly together—or to the extent that, as Clausewitz famously declared, war is only a continuation of politics by other means—then to note the inconsistency in "You shall not kill" is to state the obvious. According to the purest style of philosophy, however, the challenge is precisely to problematize the obvious. What is obvious within the scenario—whether regular or irregular, old or new—of killing humans? What "normality" justifies multiple homicide that today tends to leave us indifferent so long as that homicide is perpetrated under skies more or less geographically distant from our own? Homicide, in effect, is understood as a private crime; murder so construed still elicits interest and, sometimes, outrage. The curators at the

D'Orsay, not to mention hack reporters and communications experts, know very well that crimes committed in hate, revenge, envy, and greed revive the often esteemed figure of the great criminal, who in turn invokes an old taboo and, as such, remains a classic. This is so true that a certain transposition of the murderer onto the political plane of international intrigue retains a noteworthy allure. We know that contemporary states imitate a model at which Mafiosi excel and—in so-called times of peace—willingly rely upon a strategy for the elimination of dangerous and inconvenient persons. This model provides "secret agents" with a "license to kill" in a boundless territory that is as wide as the world. The expression "license to kill" was made famous in the Hollywood version of James Bond and corresponds to what, in more technical terms, has today come to be called *targeted killing* and that is more or less *targeted murder*. The vocabulary is modern, as is the technological rationalization of a homicide perpetrated in cold blood, but the process has an archaic flavor that revives the taste for murder already exploited by authors of detective fiction and thrillers. From the lofty accomplishments of John le Carré to the second-rate plots of Michael Crichton, a great deal of the success of literary and movie spy stories has everything to do with this archaicity [*arcaicità*], well before the accusation that the powerful are criminals cloaked in hypocrisy, which in any case counts for nothing. When the killer flushes out and kills his victim, the crime is still a crime; it is still the murder of one man by another, even if it is on commission and without passion. This is still a scene where murder retains the elementary basis of its concept and where as such "You shall not kill" maintains a meaning. That is exactly what we cannot say, however, about the contemporary theater of casual, anonymous slaughter—especially slaughter of the helpless. Here the very verb "to kill" itself loses its meaning.

WHEN KILLING IS LAWFUL
AND JUST

No matter how often it sings the praises of peace, the
Bible abounds with massacres and wars carried out
against the enemies of Israel in the name of God. The
cultural semantics of monotheistic religions are notoriously characterized by a crude and ferocious vocabulary
of violence.[1] The episode of the golden calf may serve as
an example. There an infuriated Moses shouts: "This is
the message of Yahweh, the God of Israel: 'Gird on your
sword, every man of you and quarter the camp from gate
to gate killing one his brother, another his friend, another his neighbor.'"[2] As for the treatment reserved for
enemy populations, we read in another famous passage:
"But as regards the towns of those peoples which Yahweh your God gives you as your own inheritance, you
must not spare the life of any living thing."[3] The Bible
offers up the image of a violent and punitive God who

passes down laws and disciplines, epitomized nowhere more fully than in the famous pronouncement of the Decalogue, where the Lord asserts: "For I, Yahweh your God, am a jealous God and I punish the father's fault in the sons, the grandsons, and the great-grandsons of those who hate me."[4] Certainly the quotations illustrating Deuteronomy's bellicose ideology—and the role played in it by votive extermination and total annihilation of the population (*cherem*)[5]—tragically could go on, but they are already sufficient to highlight one clear point: the very context in which the sixth Word of God appears, in its original accepted meaning as a "strong and vertical commandment handed down from above,"[6] is drenched in the language of violence and war empowered by this very verticality.

According to a classification that at this point enjoys wide consensus, the Christian tradition contains three positions about war and peace: pacifism, just war, and crusade (which can also be called holy war).[7] Put simply, we could say that the position of pacifism understands the sixth commandment as a "You shall *never* kill," the theory of the just war understands it as a prohibition against homicide that is suspended in specific circumstances, and the paradigm of holy war upends and transforms it into the fearful command, "*Kill in the name of God.*" It is a matter of fact that this last paradigm, rooted in biblical language, feeds in various modes—however perverse and evil those may be—the fundamentalist horrorism of our epoch. Today, in the literature on the phenomenon, there abound books that tellingly bear titles like *Terror in the Name of God* or *Terror in the Mind of God*.[8]

Embraced by some radical Christians in the first centuries, the theory of pacifism counts very few adherents after the work of Augustine—even though it reappears at the beginning of the sixteenth century in particularly convincing argumentation by the Christian humanist Erasmus of Rotterdam. Without a doubt, the work of Augustine of Hippo proves decisive. Augustine plucks a concept from Roman law and introduces the category of *justum bellum* into Christian thought. For Augustine, "just war" is a complex theoretical apparatus that, while looking to establish the limits and contain the excesses of war, ends up justifying it and therefore legitimizing the killing of enemies. The model becomes well established with the work of Thomas Aquinas and, with few exceptions, then passes on to the entire Christian tradition as fundamental doctrine on the rules and methods about groups of human beings to be killed. It is worth underlining that in *Summa Theologica*, Aquinas's major work, the arguments developed around the issue of war in *De bello* are reiterated in the arguments that deal directly with the sixth commandment in *De homicidio*.[9] Thomas maintains that war is just if declared by a public authority, if undertaken for a just cause—self-defense, above all—and if concluded with a peace. Invoking the sphere of law, war becomes legitimate especially when based on an ethical foundation: not all wars are just, only those that are fought according to criteria in keeping with Christian ethics. Reflecting on the undoubtedly more dreadful paradigm of the crusade or holy war, which can call up Deuteronomy's "warrior God,"[10] we deal with a schema not only more plausible but also particularly malleable in the face of a re-elaboration that substitutes a secular ethic for a religious one. In effect, after the complex theoretical and juridical vicissitudes that carry it right up to modernity, the schema of the "just war" reveals itself to be well suited to welcome the rationalistic appeal of the secular ethic. Updated to apply to the various problems of bloodbaths in progress, it still appears in actual debate on war. Michael Walzer, an American philosopher whose best-known book carries the title *Just and Unjust Wars* (1977), provides one notable example. Even more illuminating is another author's essay, "The Ethics of Killing in War,"[11] which critically discusses Walzer's positions and theoreticians of just war more generally. This is hardly the place to provide an annotated bibliography and to cite titles that are a more or less suggestive reformulation of *justum bellum*. It's enough to note that, even today, the problem is represented in terms of essentially moral justification of the act of killing. Precisely when butchery spreads on the global scene on a large scale, the commandment "You shall not kill" discovers old and new reasons to suspend itself.

TO CUT LIFE SHORT

The special law of the sixth commandment—in other words, its inability to be proposed as an absolute prohibition—finds a crucial touchstone in the absolute nature of its very object: death and its irreversibility. To kill is to mete out death. In the other commandments, life is not the issue, and the consequence of transgression is not irrecoverable. If I rob, I can restitute or repay. If I give false testimony, I can retract it. But for death— at least on the plane of earthly existence—there is no remedy. For whoever has a mortal body, to kill strikes the chord of the definitive and irrevocable. Nowhere does the commandment's inability to support *never* spring forth more clearly. The *never* sounds so loudly, in fact, that it echoes in the radicality of the *never again*. Expressed otherwise, yes, a form of the absolute still lies at the heart of the commandment, but it has to do with the mortal life of the victim: for the victim's life the effect of the homicidal act is absolute. The form of violence that tends to be identified with the very idea of violence—killing—cuts short life, precisely, by spilling blood. Significantly, in the language of Genesis, "life" and "blood" tend to be synonymous. The text offers a noteworthy philological problem relating to the first homicide committed by man. Turning to Cain, God says: "Listen to the sound of your brother's blood, crying out to me from the ground."[1] In the original Hebrew, "blood" (*damim*) is a plural word—reading, literally, "bloods." An authoritative rabbinical tradition gives the following explanation: Killing Abel, Cain also annihilates all the progeny who would have been born of Abel's blood. That is, Cain kills the future lives contained within the generative power [*potenza*] of the progenitor of a lineage. The question famously harks back to the imperative: "Be fruitful, multiply, and teem over the earth."[2] So God entrusts to man the task of perpetuating His creation through procreation, referring above all to His people: Israel. Understood as fertile blood that generates a line of descendents and populates the earth, life belongs not so much to man as to God; it recurs to God's alliance with the Hebrew people by virtue of this fertility. This theme is important not only because it projects onto an archaic screen the shadow of a biopolitical *dispositif* but also, above all, because it signals the difference between the Jewish and Christian concepts of life, even as it provides further proof of the close kinship, in the present, between the modern conviction that life is the greatest good and the Christian idea of "sacred life."

In her writing on this subject, Hannah Arendt noted that, although the Christian insistence on the sacred quality of life is a Jewish legacy, Judaism emphasizes the potential immortality of the people [*popolo*] of Israel, not the immortality of individual life. That explains why "the Decalogue enumerates the offense of murder, without any emphasis, among a number of other transgressions."[3] Whoever spills blood spills precisely the "bloods" of descendants to come, and, with a certain consistency, if Israel is to populate the earth, it is necessary for it to spill the blood of its enemies. Because Christian immortality adheres to the person, by contrast, faith in an eternal life in the heavenly realm determines "an enormously increased importance of life on earth."[4] Given that each individual is destined for eternity, so too does each individual's earthly life become sacred. According to Arendt, it is exactly this Christian conception of the sanctity of life, having traveled through to modernity by means of secularization, that has fed the modern conviction that life is the greatest good. The decline of faith in the immortality of the individual does not, however, lack consequences. Today the greatest good is not in fact the individual life, as was true in the Middle Ages, but instead "the everlasting life process of the species mankind."[5] By reconstructing the theoretical and cultural itinerary that leads "the life of the species which asserted itself," Arendt has a precise thesis in mind. We are dealing

not only with the accusation that modernity has a bi-
ologistic drift but also with an observation of its perverse denouement in the "living skeletons," reduced to
being "exemplars of the species of humankind," who
crowd the camps of Auschwitz in the mid-twentieth
century. Their survival of a condition known, up until
then, as the limit between life and death, is "naked life"
rather than life.

The category of "naked life,"[6] made famous by the current reflection on biopolitics that started with Foucault,
interests us in this case for two reasons. The first relates
to its capacity to represent the culmination of that
specifically modern parabola that not only develops a
growing obsession with "life in and for itself" through a
reconfiguration of the Christian dogma of sacred life but
that also exalts this life's autonomous and impersonal
force to the detriment of the singularity of the living being: the reasons of the singular living being succumb to
the reasons of life, to Life as such.[7] Add to this a second
concern tied to the first: in addition to its function as a
decisive category for the very definition of the field of
biopolitics, "naked life" also functions as a central category in a more recent area of discourse that seems to be
directly developed from it: bioethics. It is not in fact the
case that, in current disputes over bioethics, Christian
doctrine clashes with secular doctrine over the question
of life.[8] In this controversy, Roman Catholic argumentation repeatedly appeals to an absolute reading of the
sixth commandment and of the charge of homicide,

which it extends to suicide. Summed up in simple terms, as it relates to the so-called problem of the end of life, the thesis is well known: "To pull the plug" of a machine that keeps a human organism alive is the equivalent of homicide. A living will falls in advance into the sin of suicide; much worse is assisted suicide, which is the homicide of the one giving consent. Given that one of the strongest points of the Roman Catholic thesis is definitely the equiparation of homicide and suicide, it's worth citing here the authority of the sources. In *De Civitate Dei*, after having clarified that the commandment "*Non occides*" addresses man and also has man for its object—that, in other words, it concerns *homicdium*—Augustine pronounces suicide a sin because "whoever kills a human being, whether himself or any other, involves himself in the charge of murder."[9] Taken up by Thomas Aquinas, this judgment thenceforth remains a firm principle for all Christianity.

Reflecting on Auschwitz, Arendt had to grapple with the problem of the inapplicability of the concept of homicide to the horror of an extreme condition in which human beings had been transformed into the living dead—into, precisely, "naked life." Today, by contrast, bioethical discourse forces us to confront the problem of the applicability of the sixth commandment to a technologically produced condition in which the very threshold between life and death remains indefinite. What remains of homicide when life survives life and when a living being reduced to "latent life" becomes a scientific laboratory for a potentially infinite deferral of an end that we hesitate to call death? The Christian conception of "sacred life" and the secular concept of life as the "greatest good" perhaps can sidestep the dispute when experience still conforms to the admonition of Ecclesiastes: "There is a time to be born and a time to die."[10] But when medical technology, which already is able to produce and freeze embryos, becomes able to transform life into survival and death into an indeterminable process, the accord between these two concepts collapses altogether. What makes it collapse, significantly, is an idea that secular modernity doesn't inherit at all from Christianity but decidedly from the Enlightenment: the principle of the autonomy of the subject and the rights of the person to dispose of himself and his own life. But modernity is a rich and complex phenomenon; the strands woven into it are many and equivocal. While the modern epoch pays overall homage to the conservation of life, the rationalist thread of the free and autonomous individual (or, rather, the *person*—if we want to express it with a vocabulary that appears, among other places, in the Charter of Fundamental Rights of the European Union) puts up a tenacious resistance to the impersonal assertions of vitalism and biologism. Especially today, the living individual who is capable of self-determination continues to appear as a valid bulwark against the primacy of life itself and, moreover, as a likely repository for an aspiration to a "quality of life" that cannot coincide with "naked life."[11] If we really go in search of a heritage, we must, in this case, look to the Greek and Roman traditions. "The conviction that life without health is not worth living . . . and that suicide is a noble gesture to escape a life become burdensome,"[12] as Arendt recalls, is a legacy of the classical world. So too the model of ethics founded on the rationality of the self and self-determination, which comes from the classical world—or, rather, from the Socratic "know thyself"—and which stands in stark contrast to the Judeo-Christian model of ethics based on obedience to the commandments of God. As argued by the most discerning secular jurists who participate in today's bioethical controversy, a person who has his own life at his disposal is also, inevitably, a person who has his own death at his disposal as well.[13] Governed as it is by technological *dispositifs* that translate the right to life into *a duty to live*, to which the secular contingent replies with arguments about the *right to die*, the "end of life" becomes a truly bewildering scene. It puts into play a set of positions inspired by Christianity yet deemed heretical by the Roman Catholic Church, which claims for believers and nonbelievers alike the dignity of death (as in, for example, the work of the theologian Hans Kung).[14] Even more striking is the Christian sensibility of a philosopher like Roberta De Monticelli, who asks herself if being a person does not really mean "to bear the ultimate responsibility—because one has consciousness [*coscienza*] and freedom, an *ethos* possessed neither by a fly nor by a bean."[15] This becomes even more so when it comes to the secular profile of a rational subject, the author of free choice, who finds it repulsive to be transformed into an organism artificially adapted to survive beyond the end of real existence, put at the disposal of advanced technologies of death and life. "Naked life" essentially falls outside the self-representations through which the autonomous individual of modernity sees himself as a living being and, by extension, akin to every other living person in whom he recognizes the status of a self. Whatever meaning we give to homicide and suicide, the horizon is such that we arrive at the limit of the self but without also passing beyond it. The self who survives naked life, in fact, cannot be killed, since he already is beyond the possible sense of his own death. He is already, as it were, "indifferent"— mere vital processes installed in an organism that temporarily retains form, an anonymous force that feeds off of a once-human appearance of which it is now the counterfeit. This, precisely, is naked life—life that can linger but that no longer can be killed.

Adapting itself to the results of biotechnology, the controversy currently taking place in bioethics has drawn another extraordinary form of "life no longer able to be killed" into the scope of the sixth commandment— the frozen embryos we have already mentioned. Roman Catholic doctrine declares that destroying them is homicide. It is worth underlining that, even though the criterion of "sacred life" here shifts to the pole of "birth," the discourse does not, as usual, focus on the female body as the heterogoverned [*eterogestito*] theater for the prevention or interruption of pregnancy. It focuses instead on an organism in a germinal state that is produced and situated outside the uterus. As the protocellular phase of the species *homo*, the frozen embryo in effect seems to constitute an ultimate challenge for a version of "You shall not kill" that wants to bind itself exceptionally to the "never." Extraordinarily invoking the absolute version in this case, the prohibition against killing a human being is pushed to the injunction against killing even the frozen cells that might bring one into being. Will it be— will it be born—ever? Will we therefore preserve forever this embryo to which the technology of freezing promises a duration—(a life?)—that is more or less eternal? And, if, in contrast to man, the frozen embryo escapes the very condition of mortality, in what sense would we be able to kill, to violently cut off its life, to mete out death to it? These and other questions clearly demonstrate how the whole picture is marked by a kind of excess, by a will to application that, precisely by deciding to take the commandment in its absolute and peremptory form, pushes it beyond the setting that usually has guaranteed its meaning. Instead of the living individual— able to be killed because already alive, born of woman and irremediably mortal—the subject here put in play is, quite beyond its acquisition of an artificial immortality, a kind of "unliving naked life" ["*nuda-vita-non-ancora-in-vita*"] that renders useless the basic coordinates with which tradition has described homicide since the time of Cain and Abel.

Between the Christian meaning of "sacred life" and the current Roman Catholic tendency to identify sacred life with naked life, there is a link that Arendt perhaps helps us understand, though not without astonishment. If, in fact, we are hardly surprised that the paradigm of the subject's self-determination holds no sway in the face of a doctrine inspired by obedience to the commandments of God, we are somewhat surprised that an uncommon zeal for complete obedience to the sixth commandment should oblige it to test its absoluteness in a technologically produced setting constituted by various forms of naked life. To this we must add that the same authoritative Christian sources often cited to maintain this operation—whether Augustine or Thomas—simultaneously provide an equally authoritative reference for the theories of "just wars" we have already mentioned. It bears repeating that the modern doctrine of the autonomous, rational subject does not arrive at different conclusions about the permissibility of killing in war or in the name of the State, even though it cites very different sources of argumentation. The modern subject, who replaces obedience to God's commandments with the obligation to obey rational laws, remains a substantially belligerent subject, Kant's proposal of *pace perpetua* notwithstanding. "You shall not kill" is a principle that the autonomous individual of modernity recognizes as an obligation in his own conscience, but when it comes to war, he continues to trigger the old *dispositif* of self-release. With the exception of the few Christian classics of radical pacifism, in contemporary culture conscientious objection to military service can therefore call upon a theoretical framework supported by rationalism. "You shall not kill" applies, essentially, only to the individual conscience.

A WEAK COMMANDMENT

The sixth commandment appears a weak commandment no matter from what cultural vantage point you
look at it. Not weak because, in private or in war, men
continue to kill one another. (They continue to steal, give
false testimony, and violate other imperatives of the
Decalogue as well.) No: it is weak *per se* because of
the inconsistency of its conceptual framework and the
contradictions that run through it historically. Even its
recent adaptation to the parameters of the bioethical
controversy, where it presents itself as a final attempt to
make the prohibition against killing absolute, ends up
dragging the commandment toward a field in which its
application weakens its meaning. In the concrete experience of the living, a dogma of the sanctity of life produces heartless and paradoxical results: pushed to its
maximum abstraction, it allows, among other things, the
ethics of truth to supplant the ethics of charity.[1] As

public opinion has today intuited, the infinitely deferred and technologically inscrutable threshold between life and death—such as the virtual immortality of the frozen embryo—not only subtracts a traditional point of force in the application of "You shall not kill" but also arrives at the question of the very meaning of the human. The homicidal act that inaugurates human history with Cain's shocking gesture nearly finds, in this case, its counterpoise [*contrapasso*]. Although some now hold that the prohibition against killing may extend even to animals and take into account the biblical question about their slaughter, when it comes to *homicidium* it is only man (*homo*) who is spoken of.

IN THE BEGINNING

The problem of the double beginning of the human race is one of the many problems for interpretation posed by the account of Genesis. Born not of woman but created by God on the sixth day, Adam and Eve live in the Garden of Eden in a state that knows no sorrow, no toil, and, above all, no death. Already freed from the human condition of being born an infant, Edenic humanity is also missing the fundamental characteristic recognized as human by nearly all cultures: mortality. As in ancient Greece, in the prehistoric time before Pandora's box was opened, there is no death in earthly paradise. A homicide in this scene would thus be unthinkable: however you may want to interpret it, the first sin is not in fact a violent act and does not spill blood. Christian tradition will call it "original sin" and, departing from an Augustinian interpretation of Pauline doctrine, will make it hereditary for the whole human race. Jewish tradition, by contrast, understands it as a sin that stands at the origin of man himself—that, in a certain sense, giving rise to man as a mortal creature who inhabits the world. It thus becomes possible to kill him, and, in effect, it is a homicide that commences the history of man—as irremediably human—following the expulsion from the Garden of Eden. Cain, born of woman, establishes the human race by killing his innocent brother. Founder of cities, Cain is also progenitor of a lineage that makes for itself community and culture, nation and history. He is the seed of Israel. According to the biblical narrative of origin, at the beginning of man—a human being so marvelous that he is created in the image of God—there is a murder that consumes itself in its own blood. Cain and Abel, two brothers: already a portent of that perfect armed confrontation—ultimately balanced and definitively bellicose—in which we will see the brothers Jacob and Esau as protagonists. In the Decalogue, Arendt reminds us, homicide is counted, without special note, among many other crimes. All the same, a murder has the sad honor of launching human history. Cain is the first to spill blood.

A similarly bloody imaginary also characterizes the account of the origin of the human race from classical antiquity. However different they may be, two essential matrices of the West—Judeo-Christian and Greek (or, if you prefer to phrase it in the famous formula of Leo Strauss, Jerusalem and Athens)[1]—converge in their emphasis on the exemplarity of the blood crime. It is worth noting, however, that there is no principle analogous to the sixth commandment in Greek culture and its social codes. The homeland of Plato and Aristotle does not reflect on the prohibition against killing in any special way. It does, however, pay particular attention to the phenomenon that the commandment presupposes: Man kills man. Drawn in various ways from myth and tragedy, the theme is essentially tied to the story of origins, that is, to the total collection of histories and legends produced by the Greek imaginary to narrate the origin of man himself. As such, it in every sense emerges from the mythologeme of autochthony, according to which the human race, born from the earth, is composed exclusively of male warriors who kill one another. This portrait presents many points of interest. In the archaic Greek imaginary, the human that distinguishes itself from gods and beasts explicitly arises as a prototype of a masculine sex that, in turn, specializes in intraspecies slaughter. In other words, humanity is born together with multiple homicide. As Pierre Vidal-Naquet notes: "Autochthony is a mythic procedure that eliminates the role played by women in originating the human species and that makes it possible for men to establish themselves as warrior fraternities."[2] This masculinist vision is not reserved only to the mythologeme of autochthony. In other stories of the origin of the human race, including the already cited myth of Pandora, the presence of women comes chronologically

late. In Greece, man is born a warrior who is characterized by brute force and who is genetically predisposed
to kill his own kind, who in turn are also embodied in a
masculine body. The warrior virtues celebrated in the *Iliad*, in which Hellenic civilization is founded in the
glorification of the slaughter of heroes, refers precisely
to this tradition. Killing is, so to speak, an ordinary
gesture for a culture that positions the archetype of a
masculine killer—bloody and avenging—at its very
origin and that develops a juridical culture around
homicide for which the Homeric poems supply the essential framework.[3] Obviously that does not mean that
the Greek world does not distinguish between war and
normal human affairs, but it does at least mean that
it gets rid of the contradiction internal to the Judeo-
Christian matrix, which must reconcile the absolute
prohibition against homicide with the legitimization of
war. More than the supreme crime, homicide is for
the Greeks—in battle as in everyday life—just one of
the many evils (*kakà*) that befall mortals (in this case, a
bloody way to lose one's life by getting killed by another). In battle such a death strikes down life in its throb-
bing vitality, and it is merciless. Homer describes it for us
in the *Iliad*:

> The bronze spear went straight through and came out
> beneath his brain, splitting the white bones. Erymas'
> teeth came flying out and both his eyes filled with

blood. He gasped, spewing blood through his mouth and nostrils, and the black cloud of death came down over him.[4]

We would do well to recall that this is not a life destined for procreation and for the immortality of a chosen people. Nor is it a sacred life made thus by the eternity of the individual soul embodied in it. It is instead a form of existence that is experienced as purely human and that belongs to the order of the ephemeral, the fragile, and the transitory. No duty of self-preservation depends on it; there's only the shudder of its inexorable loss revealed in advance by the violent blow of homicide. Having faith in his promised destiny of glory, a warrior like Achilles is obviously persuaded: his specialty consists of killing the greatest number of men before being killed himself. Insofar as it is a specialized sphere of killing, war itself is just an intensive dramatization on a wider plane of what in everyday life and custom already regulates homicide: the model of "blood avenger" or, if we turn back to the Bible, the law of retaliation. As Deuteronomy states, "You are to show no pity. Life for life, eye for eye, tooth for tooth, hand for hand, foot for foot."[5] It seems typical of archaic societies that, in the Greek version, the model requires that the murderous act be read as an offense to the family and tribe of the one killed and that the mechanism of reprisal be its primary rule. Whoever has killed must be killed, and it is the relatives of the victim who must shoulder the responsibility, according to a principle of fairness and proportion.

On this subject, it is useful to point out that public institutions in the Greek *polis* do not neutralize the tribal system of retribution; they inherit and administer it. Even in the classical period, homicide is perceived by the political community as an essentially private crime: Those responsible for judicial action against the murderer—that is, the kin of the victim—can pardon him completely instead of demanding his death, as the fundamental logic of the vendetta demands, but only if they also exact monetary compensation (the "blood price"). Judges and the laws of the city play an important role in the historical development of archaic Greek law (as Plato, among others, theorizes in a detailed survey of cases in Book IX of the *Laws*).[6] In substance, however, homicide remains an issue whose roots sink deep in the ties of kinship or, if you wish, in the sphere of the natural group. As Émile Benveniste notes: "Homicide in general is not punished as such in ancient codes. In order to be punishable it was necessary for the murder to affect a man of the group: morality stopped at the frontier of the natural group."[7] In other words, in symptomatic congruence with the myth of autochthony and with warrior brotherhood, kinship is the original and foundational scene of the homicidal act. No one can represent that better than Oedipus.

Everyone knows the story of Jocasta's unfortunate son, the parricide. Oedipus killed a man because of a quarrel at a crossroad (a question of virility—it had to do with right of way!), but he did not know that man was his father. All the rest—the throne of Thebes, incest, the children born of his mother's womb—were nothing but a consequence of this act. From the Greek perspective, he is guilty of parricide no matter what, and the stain of his guilt washes over Thebes like a plague. Here the term "parricide" obviously stands for a precise type of crime: Oedipus has killed his father. He is guilty of *patroctonia*. Philologists tell us that the etymology of the Latin *parricidium*, however, does not explicitly allude to the father figure: it instead denotes the murder of a free man. From Greek to Latin, or perhaps even earlier, the meaning changes. The killing of the father by the son, who almost forgets his primal scene, becomes the general paradigm of homicide. In Greece, where killing calls into question the very definition of the human, homicide nevertheless speaks the language of strict kinship and warrior brotherhood.

Oedipus lends himself in effect to the narrative of crimes committed in families. Weighed down since birth by an oracle that destines him to kill his father Laius, Oedipus does murder him, not knowing his identity, but not before evading his parents' murderous plan for him earlier in his infancy. In the lineage of the Labdacids, to which both Oedipus and Laius belong, murder reserved for one's own blood is a constant that knows few exceptions. Protagonists of one of the most famous legends of autochthony, the Labdacids descend from the line of the

Spartans: warriors sown in the earth and born from dragon's teeth (absolutely not from woman). We are therefore in the presence of a paradigmatic case in which the full range of homicidal practice is returned to a single common nucleus: Autochthonous warriors who kill one another, the Spartans discover in Oedipus the haunting champion of a homicide accomplished within the circle of his own blood. The myth suggests to us that homicidal experience is so consubstantial with man that it roots itself precisely there where the human is most immediately and, as it were, physically closest to his own origin: the narrow kinship of his own blood relatives. Parricide and incest certainly belong to the tale of Oedipus, but, more than functioning as universal characters in a developmental stage of the psyche—as Freud would have it—they testify to the particular way in which the Greek imaginary emphasizes endogamous relations in its projection of the evil of homicide on the family. In the final analysis, this suggests not only that spilled blood calls out for more spilled blood but, above all, that spilled blood is always one's *own*: the closest and most like ours. Through Oedipus, in the Greece that speaks the language of myth and tragedy, the horror of homicide fixes its gaze on the most profound, vital relation. And it is a horror that irrupts in this relation—which is the prototype and matrix of every human relation—as a contagious filth, a disease, a stain.

Blood calls out for blood. But blood sullies, soils, stains. The ancient warrior, who strikes with hacking weapons at close range, has a realistic experience of this phenomenon. In the Homeric world—in a world where warriors cover themselves in the filth of others' blood every day—such a stain assumes a character that is substantially material, physical, and tangible. They see it and smell its stink. Whoever kills thus also dirties himself. He therefore must wash himself, purify himself with ablutions that, in time, tend to assume an appearance of ritual. Even if his action lies beyond social and moral judgments, homicide remains impure. The warrior, in other words, kills—"war has to do with killing," writes Elias Canetti; "its first aim is enemy dead."[8] The warrior soils himself with blood and dust, which is exactly what befalls his victim. Similar to a disease, a plague, a *miasma*, the filth renders both warrior and victim contagious. Thus must the warrior wash himself, and the dead body must be burned. Thus may the intraspecies carnage start all over again: cleansed bodies of warriors, more blood that mixes with dust, more dead bodies. And more purifications: the cycle is short and follows the rhythms of war. On the other hand, evidently, in the original scene of the family of which the saga of the Labdacids is a model, the cycle is less brief. The stain lingers long, the contagion is a genetic inheritance, and the purification turns out to be complex. Doesn't the dreadful stain pass from Laius to Oedipus and then to his brother-sons Eteocles and Polynices and his daughter-sister Antigone? And, after the parricide, isn't there a fratricide and then in the end, as Sophocles tells it, an impure corpse that gets in the way? As experts know, these questions swarm over the specialized studies of the figure of Oedipus (according to a range of themes that run from the pure and impure, to the sacred, to the scapegoat, to *pharmakon*, and beyond). We, by contrast, will be satisfied with a simpler discourse. In the Theban legend, in essence, Oedipus provides the illustration of a homicidal act that, being carried out against his own blood, turns that same blood into a vehicle of contamination. He never escapes the circle of that homicide, and at the *center* of that circle—its shape and sustenance—is the *proprium*. That we are dealing with a parricide—and not a matricide—reveals another side of the issue that is hardly accidental but rather essential.

If it is true that matricidal Orestes takes part in the legend of the founding of Athens, the Greek imaginary on homicide as an act tied to the origins of humanity—as also happens in the Bible, for the most part—definitely requires masculine protagonists. It's worth repeating: in war as in the family, only men do the business of killing. As expressed through the character of Oedipus, war, parricide, and fratricide all are closely interrelated. The myth of autochthon tells the same story as the myth of the unfortunate son of Laius: Bloody male hands are at the heart of a representation that cannot speak of the human without also describing men who kill other men. That man kills man, that Cain initiates human history in the Bible by murdering Abel, is, in other words, an obvious logical premise for the text of the sixth commandment. The figure of the murderer precedes the prohibition that enjoins him "not to kill." Is it always, then, a warrior, a son, a brother who stands at the beginning? Is it obligatory that the homicide of a blood relative must found various human cultures and even, in the famous case of Romulus and Remus, the political realm itself?

HOMO NECANS

Scholars from various disciplines currently hold the opinion that homicide is an anthropological constant, a distinctive trait of the universally understood human spirit, a bloody trademark of the species. It appears we must say much the same for war as a permanent factor in the history of man and for the transcultural presence of vendetta in archaic societies. Tribal avenger or warrior—and founder of community—the masculine figure resides in the stories of the origin in many versions, with a certain documentable persistence. And when research like this takes up the evolutionary model and turns to looking into the primitive stage of the hunt, it only ends up accentuating his homicidal characteristics.

In the 1960s, the anthropologist Walter Burkert, an expert in antiquity and religion, published a book with the eloquent title *Homo Necans*.[1] We could translate it as "man who kills" or "man the killer," but certainly the Latin is more effective. Richly clad in that language's authority, we immediately intuit the wordplay: the renowned *homo sapiens* is *homo necans*. To employ a definition of a philosophical type, the rational animal is an animal that kills: his specialties, the distinctive characteristics of the species, are the capacity for *logos* and killing. According to Burkert's evolutionist model, this fact would find its roots in the Paleolithic era, when, having chosen a carnivorous diet, man became a hunter. Anticipated, among others, by authors such as Erasmus of Rotterdam and Thomas More—who didn't yet have the evolutionist justification for it and bitterly condemned it—the hunter has a complicated history that Burkert's thesis allows us to simplify: the practice of hunting developed, in man, a predatory instinct based on the killing of animals and on a taste for blood. This in turn changed him inexorably into an aggressive subject, driven to expend his homicidal energy upon his own species. The drive to kill, vital for a hunting culture, here changes its object—or, better, it expands to include even individuals of the species to which the hunter belongs. *Homo necans* kills those who resemble him. Like wolves, leopards, and other carnivores, yes, he is a living being that kills other living creatures to eat their meat, but, above all, he is homicidal. The outcome of the path taken by the hunter is murder.

Beyond its specific content, Burkert's thesis covers an area—however vast and uneven it may be—that is very important to twentieth-century thought. Today we encounter various disciplines that could be grouped under the generic rubric of the "human sciences" and that converge in rereading man and his history in terms of a constitutive aggressiveness that's often traced back to sexuality. To stay with the most famous instances, psychoanalysis above all speaks of aggressiveness, starting with Freud, although we owe the most extreme theory to Melanie Klein, who underlines the destructiveness of aggression and theorizes it as an original, instinctual dimension that is substantially structural and already present in infancy. Ethnology, as embodied in the authoritative work of Konrad Lorenz, speaks of aggressive drives directed at individuals of the same species. Religious studies, for its part, discovers a fundamental turning point in the theories of René Girard, who notoriously insists on intraspecies violence as the foundation of the sacred.[2] All in all, when this vast current in late modernity reflects on human beings, it thinks of them—to a great extent and with all necessary distinctions—as naturally aggressive and destructive subjects who will kill one another unless inhibited by social norms. As Darwin suggested, life—not so much the life of a single living being but rather life in itself—is a struggle. As we already have noted, the complex business of modernity puts us in a position to celebrate a life force that, in turn, contests head-on the Enlightenment paradigm of the rational subject and his dreams of autonomy and transparency. Hunter or warrior, tribal father or blood avenger—we just have to change the point of observation or the discursive protocol—the aggressive subject, absolutely of male gender, projects his archetype on the beginning of human history and declares solidarity with that in which contemporary man is also still called to recognize himself. Killing is in our nature, also known as culture. Our essence is violence.

From a certain stylistic and methodological point of view, we are dealing here with a sort of feedback loop. More worrisome than this, however, is the epochal dominance of a destructive conception of humanity that, theorized in the name of biologizing realism, closes the door on any alternative conception of humanity, branding it naive in advance. In other words, it is extremely difficult today to think a subject that constitutes itself originarily through peace and altruism, much less to discover an imaginary that can describe and transmit that subject. Condemning war in 1515, Erasmus could still denounce the zoological anomaly of the human race: "When was it ever heard that an hundred thousand brute beasts were slain at one time fighting and tearing one another: which thing men do full oft and in many places?"[3] Erasmus could also maintain that man, by his very nature—who, in contrast to wild beasts, is given neither fangs nor claws—is poorly adapted to kill: Nothing in his naked, unarmed body destines him to battle and the practice of violence. Today a discourse such as this— which some of his more intrepid followers might still propose—would be laughingly dismissed as naive pacifism and useless utopianism. For the aggressive subject, who so thoroughly adapts himself to war, war is more than just the original stage on which murder loses its character of crime. The theory of the "just war," defended on moral grounds though it may be, doesn't even apply in this context. Killing is absolutely natural, and, when the sovereign orders it in the name of the State, it's legitimate and normal.

In the history of the political figures assumed by the aggressive subject in modernity, a place of honor is obviously reserved for Thomas Hobbes and his famous formula *homo homini lupus*. According to Hobbes, men are characterized by a natural and extreme selfishness that leads them to kill one another. As the author of *Leviathan* argues, everyone is moved by a survival instinct (*conatus*) that makes him see in all others not only dangerous rivals to beat but also obstacles to eliminate. The result is *bellum omnium contra omnes*, war of all against all. With a clever theoretical maneuver, war is thus cast as a "state of nature" and becomes foundational for the concepts of humanity and politics alike. The war in question here does not, however, correspond to the traditional theory and practice of war: it does not consist of a conflict between groups, tribes, nations, or even more or less regular armies. It consists instead of a horizontal distribution of the practice of intraspecies homicide among individuals. Isolated from everyone else—brought forth like a mushroom, according to the curious expression of Hobbes in *De cive*[4]—and lacking in brothers or family, the warrior stands alone. In reality, we can't even speak of a warrior here, only of a murderer in the pure state, a being without kin or brothers. He kills whatever others there may be solely and exclusively in his own name. Projected on the background of a hypothetical state of nature, the scene is notoriously paradoxical, but it at least has the value of furnishing an effective self-representation for that individual who looks to assert and impose himself in the first place, who is therefore genetically aggressive, and whose absolute essence, to quote Emanuel Lévinas, lies in "the brutal perseverance of beings in their being."[5] In one of Dostoyevsky's most famous novels, Ivan Karamazov—descendant of a tribe of murderers and parricide *in pectore*—uses the eloquent expression "thirst for life."[6] If the rationalist mask [*maschera*] of the modern subject continues to justify war, his vitalist mask consigns him to a congenital destructiveness that makes war the true theater for his self-realization.

YOU SHALL NEVER KILL

In 1984, delivering a speech commemorating peace in Europe, Emmanuel Lévinas underlines how the West lacks "a sensibility in which the scandal of murder is not suppressed even when the violence is rationally necessary."[1] If the vitalist mask of the subject holds war inevitable and even healthy, the rationalist mask holds it all the more necessary to secure peace. Intuiting that the two masks demonstrate a substantial complicity and distrusting an idea of peace that continues to be based on war, Lévinas elaborates a radical critique of violence that is based on an atypical reading of the sixth commandment—or, better still, of the Word of God in terms of imperative verbs. According to the philosopher, "You shall not kill" must be understood as an absolute prohibition that provides for no exceptions and always, in whatever circumstances, points to the outrage of homicide. The thesis is both unusual and anomalous. Proposed by a thinker whose matrix is explicitly Jewish, it sets itself above all in contrast to the biblical representation of a God who guides his people to war, to the annihilation of enemies, and to vengeance with an especially blood-thirsty accent. Lévinas's Judaism—according to which, as we recalled at the beginning, "the entire Torah, in its minute descriptions, is concentrated in the 'Thou Shalt not kill' that the face of the other signifies"[2]—in effect has characteristics of extreme originality and presents itself not only as a radical shift with respect to whatever tradition might legitimate homicide in the name of law, religion, and politics but also, and above all, as an escha-tological vision of peace that "breaks with the totality of wars and empires."[3] In a vision of this sort, no founda-tional role is assigned to violence. For Lévinas, the pro-hibition against killing is so absolute that one can no longer postulate a logical priority for homicide. "You shall not kill," understood as an utterance that comes directly from the face of the other in the "face-to-face" encounter between two unique beings, may provoke the "temptation of homicide," but the event itself inscribes its prohibition.

Chapter 32 of Genesis, writes Lévinas, recounts an epi-sode in the life of Jacob, in which he is upset by the news that his brother Esau is marching on him at the head of "four hundred men." The biblical text continues: "Jacob was greatly afraid and distressed." The renowned eleventh-century rabbinical commentator Rashi explains that Jacob was afraid of his own death but even more anguished by being obliged to kill. According to Lévinas, we must question ourselves about the meaning of this anguish if we are to arrive at an eschatological vision of peace. As the ancients already noted and as a modern version emphasizes even more, fear of one's own death has in fact no need of special examination. I want to live, says a more or less rational subject who has "thirst for life": the being in me wants to persevere in its being, the *conatus* for survival imposes itself on the "I" as a natural law of life itself. According to this law, therefore, Jacob would have to kill Esau, who, armed, threatens him with death. He would have to kill him, that is, out of legitimate self-defense even before the impending war drags him into its logic. Instead he agonizes precisely because of this *obligation* to kill. This anguish, comments Lévinas, is already an effect of the "You shall not kill" communicated from one face to the other, in the encounter between two unique beings who look at each other "face to face." And it is precisely that which overcomes the survival drive of the "I" here represented by Jacob. According to Lévinas, before the face of the other signifies the prohibition against killing, there remains nothing of the "I." The Lévinasian interpretation of "You shall not kill" here appears in all its paradoxicality. To cast off its traditional aggressive essence, the "I" must *not* already be there on the scene but appear only through the vulnerability of the face of the other that summons it by saying "you."

In the Italian *non uccidere*, as in many other cases, including the original Hebrew, there is a "you" (*tu*) that risks remaining implicit, overlooked, unseen. French, the language in which Lévinas writes, avoids that risk: "*Tu ne tueras point*." "You shall not kill," according to the philosopher, is not only what the face of the other says; it is, first of all, what originarily establishes the "I" through the "you" pronounced by this word. The Lévinasian critique of the centrality of the subject aims, first of all, to dismantle the notion of an "I" that, like a wild beast struggling for existence, produces the hellish conflict between egoism and the political *dispositifs* that regulate it. Because the interdiction against killing takes on an absolute meaning, the "I" absolutely cannot be the first personage to enter the scene. On this stage, characterized by two embodied singularities obliged to gaze upon each other "face to face," there is, above all, the face of the other, without defense, that announces the humanity of man—the inception, so to speak, to every face of the human race—in terms of vulnerability and exposure. "Moses and the prophets preoccupied themselves not with the immorality of the soul but with the poor, the widow, the orphan and the stranger," writes Lévinas.[4] The other is my neighbor, whom I do not yet know but whom I encounter in the uniqueness of his face. In other words, the other is not necessarily Esau—brother in arms, figure of symmetry between brother-warriors, and rather suspect as an authentic foundation for peace. The other, in the "face to face" that prohibits even a legitimate defense, is above all vulnerable and helpless.

At one point Lévinas declares that what he says of the face of the other probably corresponds to what the Christian says about the face of Christ.[5] Most human and mortally wounded, Christ would therefore be the other who looks at us "face to face." Even though the speeches of Jesus of Nazareth may present a certain ambiguity when it comes to an unconditional condemnation of violence, it is worth adding that the most original aspect of his preaching seems to fit easily within the horizon of meaning outlined by Lévinas. And certainly it is the case that some Christian authors of the early centuries took up the invitation to love one's enemies and turn the other cheek, taking the imperative "You shall not kill" so literally that they arrived at an extreme pacifism that included even a prohibition on joining the army. The strong Jewish background of Lévinas's thought, coupled, above all, with a inferred wariness of the Christian tradition, push him toward a Jewish ethic of peace that tended to ignore Jesus. He cannot avoid, however, the comparison with the biblical precept that the Nazarene takes up with great conviction and places at the heart of his message: "You must love your neighbor as yourself."[6] We witness here, in fact, two types of radicalization. As regards the problematic of the sixth commandment, Jesus turns to his habitual phrase, "but I say unto you," to amplify the reach of the precept expressed in the Torah in a significant way: "You have learnt how it was said: *You must love your neighbor* and hate your enemy. But I say this unto you: love your enemies and pray for those who persecute you."[7] Lévinas, by contrast, radicalizes the precept by providing a different version. "You will love your neighbor; he is yourself," writes the philosopher.[8] The selfish foundation of the precept—the "I" who loves the other on the basis of the love that he has for himself— here gets replaced by a fundamental principle that raises the other up as the standard. The thesis is entirely consistent with the complex framework of Lévinasian reflection: in the imperative "You shall not kill," as well as in the precept "Love your neighbor; he is yourself," there is no "I" who might precede the other and who might not be established by "you." Lévinas wagers on the possibility of an originary peace that, in the destitution of the subject and its aggressive substance, restores the prohibition against homicide to an absolute law. The commandment here neither suspends itself nor leaves open wide, empty spaces. "You shall *never* kill," in substance, says the Word in which the Torah is realized. Shifted from the verticality of the divine commandment to the horizontal plane of human faces who gaze upon one another, the injunction is valid everywhere and always.

THE SEX OF CAIN

And if Cain had been a woman? The hypothesis is obviously absurd, and it is so for more than one reason. Even though Eve has an important role in the Edenic scene of sin that establishes humanity as a mortal species, the homicidal and fratricidal act that initiates human history provides for no woman. Something analogous happens to Pandora, the first woman according to Hesiod, from whose belly is born death in addition to other ills for the human race: the lineage that then descends from her is exclusively male, often brothers or those united in the warrior brotherhoods, whose specialty is to butcher one another. Passing over the male hunter whom Burkert used as the model for *homo necans*, we may here recapitulate the question with the incisive words of Jacques Derrida: "Over centuries of war and costumes, hats, uniforms, soutanes, warriors, colonels, generals, partisans, strategists, politicians, professors, political theoreticians, theologians, in vain would you look for a figure of a woman."[1] This does not mean, of course, that women do not kill. To be convinced that they do, it would be enough to cast a glance at the Uffizi's famous painting of *Judith Slaying Holofernes* by Artemisia Gentileschi or to reread Euripides' *Medea*. As the earliest narratives assure us, women kill too. Large parts of the chronicles and the popular imaginary that take up homicide are occupied by the woman murderer and avenger, the "dark lady" thirsty for blood—*vamp* comes from vampire—and, above all, even today, the terrifying mother-infanticide. The D'Orsay exhibition "Crime and Punishment" mentioned above takes account of this fact with a certain justified insistence. In terms of private crime, women have played their part for a long time, earning themselves their deserved punishment. In terms of war, even though we already have seen women protagonists in the misogynous myth of the Amazons, the phenomenon of women in war is fairly recent; it is, for the most part, the perhaps inauspicious result of the slow process of emancipation that finally has admitted women to military service as well as to other responsibilities earlier reserved for only men. But neither of these issues shifts the fundamental question. As Derrida reminds us, the structures of meaning through which we recognize the West—or, if you prefer, recognize the human specialty of homicide, to say nothing of homicide's cultural and political function in the vision of the world as it now exists—insist upon the centrality of the male. Certainly Cain had sisters, but he, not they, spilled the first blood. Romulus and Remus belonged to the strong sex.

Among the twentieth-century theories who reread man and his history in terms of constitutive aggression, more than a few also tend to cast the process of civilization in terms of progressive introjection of the social and cultural *dispositifs* that inhibit the violent instincts of the individual. Following along with the famous thesis of Norbert Elias,[2] it generally has been emphasized that concentrating the monopoly on violence in institutional hands corresponds, in everyday life, to *civilized* behavior of subjects who spontaneously control their aggressive instincts because they have introjected the norms of prohibition. In essence—this thesis says—we are genetically violent, but, with modernity and its *dispositifs* of regulation, we have learned self-control and have become less archaic or, as some would say, less barbaric.

"Our education totally opposes murder, violence, and abuse, and these precepts are so powerfully inculcated, so profoundly and completely absorbed, that they have become a constitutive part of the physical and psychological equipment of the normal man."[3] This quotation, hardly lacking in critical tone, appears in a book by Giovanni De Luna, in which the author, as a historian, reflects on the horrors of contemporary war and, in particular, on the insulting treatment reserved for the body of the slain enemy. The phenomenology of twentieth-century carnage—and the actual tendencies to intensify the slaughter and harm—hardly harmonize with the thesis of the civilizing process. It is relevant to this problem that the *normal* man, whose *forma mentis* has introjected the prohibition against killing, easily can be transformed into a warrior capable of unspeakable massacres. One of the solutions that has gained a certain credibility among scholars of the subject insists on the traumatic character of the scene of war and, within that context, proposes evidence of the traces of civilization that more or less persist in the attitude of combatants. On this subject, De Luna cites observations of military historians on the behavior and emotions of contemporary soldiers when, after exercises against fictitious targets, they find themselves in the bloody reality of battle: they note the soldiers' basic fear "is not of being killed so much as of killing."[4] Surprisingly, therefore, we once again encounter Lévinas's principle—almost to the letter! According to what some experts say, the ordinary soldier, like Jacob, fears for his life, but he also fears even more that he *perhaps* may be obliged to kill. (Technology distances the victims, mostly struck down en masse, from their killers.) The real surprise comes, however, in further comments about specific details of this phenomenon. De Luna always reminds us that we are talking about "an extreme pathology that reflects on the body of the male combatant, giving rise to his sudden feminization."[5] The thesis is clear: If the "normal" and properly civilized man is called upon to kill but is too afraid to do it—and if, beyond that, he feels distress—then that means that his masculine essence has given way to feminine nature. Invoked with the typical arrogance of Jungian jargon, gender stereotypes shuffle the cards and confuse the discourse as soon as they enter the scene.

When we reflect on sexual difference, gender stereotypes are always in play, no matter what: As not only feminist thought has argued for a long while, it is absolutely impossible to talk about "masculine" and "feminine" outside of cultural frameworks or, if you wish, outside the language that gives the terms meaning and therefore control every discourse on the subject. On one hand, the problem lies in demonstrating in detail various historical contexts that produce this language and, on the other, in emphasizing that, in terms of the practice and representation of violence, the picture presents a noteworthy continuity. From Cain onward, tradition has conceived the murderer of his own kind as masculine. Above all, in more recent times, modeling the entire human species on the masculine, it has conceived of an aggressive subject predisposed to homicide. No matter how complicated and historicized, the picture remains the same. Even the thesis of the civilizing process, which confers internal, inhibiting restraints upon the aggressor, continues to open up theaters of intraspecies butchery in which those restraints must, of necessity, be loosened. Today, as in the past, the sixth commandment is a rule prized for its social usefulness but full of reasoned exceptions. To a real man, at least in certain circumstances, "You shall not kill" sounds unvirile, womanish, false.

To a woman, for reasons that not only feminism has illustrated, this commandment sounds instead like an almost obvious imperative. Most recent feminist thought, in its various articulations and traditions, inclines toward pacifism, and it has no difficulty in furnishing testimony to support it. The ranks of the heroines of peace are vast. The place of honor customarily goes to Antigone, the unfortunate daughter of Oedipus who rejects the homicidal and martial destiny of the Labdacids in Sophocles' tragedy with a pronouncement that has become justifiably famous: "I wasn't born to hate one with the other, but to love both together."[6] Virginia Woolf, on the eve of the Second World War, deserves no less attention for a famous passage in *Three Guineas* that emphasizes how men derive from combat "some glory, some necessity, some satisfaction in fighting which we have never felt or enjoyed."[7] The category of "foreignness" [*estraneità*], which is found in so many other women authors that the list would be too long to provide here, proves the most meaningful and convincing to take up as the crux of the problem we are examining. If it is indeed true that gender stereotypes necessarily establish the framework of the discourse—even of our own here—it is also true that, by excluding women, the masculine monopoly in the sphere of violence gives women at least the advantage of putting to good use their foreignness to slaughter and of claiming a fitting distance from the aggressive subject who holds sway. In other words, women do not easily recognize themselves in the phenomenology of the warrior and his dubious virtues. Nor do they comfortably see themselves in the model of an "I" who insists on celebrating independence and self-sufficiency. Experts in the drama of birth rather than of death, women know that no one arrives in the world alone and that existence is structurally dependent, often off balance, and in need of care. Among the various feminist theories that mark current reflections on violence there prevails the disposition to conceive of the human condition in terms of a constitutive relation with the other, a relation characterized by vulnerability, dependence, and precariousness.[8] Here the infant often functions as the archetype of a human race which refuses to start off with homicidal acts and instead realistically narrates its beginning in each individual's arrival in the world as a new start. Thus does the "I" get stripped of its narcissistic dreams and its nightmares about being overcome while on the primary plane the ethical and ontological function of "you" stands out in a new form. We here find a "you" that, however differently from the one invoked by Lévinas in "You shall not kill," nevertheless also quickly avoids provoking the temptation to kill and its imaginary.

In the last analysis, the fundamental issue—one that not even Lévinas escapes—is the claim that a homicide or, at least, the temptation of it necessarily inhabits any discourse on the human race and the representations of its origin. Significantly, however, this is only the masculine version of history. There are perhaps other possible narratives of humanity that do not spring from fratricide, parricide, and warrior lineages. There are certainly philosophies of the human that do not postulate her natural aggressiveness. And most symptomatically, there is a longing for future political orders in which peace is not the temporary result of war.

The sister of Cain and, so too, Antigone and many others allow us to imagine them.

NOTES

POINT OF DEPARTURE

1. Avot de-Rabbi Nathan, *The Fathers According to Rabbi Nathan*, trans. Judah Goldin (New Haven, Conn.: Yale University Press, 1983), 125–126. Translation modified.

2. *Catechism of the Catholic Church*, 2nd ed. (Chicago: University of Loyola Press, 1994), 502.

3. Exodus 20.2–17; Deuteronomy 5.6–21. [All biblical quotations in both essays are taken from *The Jerusalem Bible* (Garden City, N.Y.: Doubleday: 1966).—Trans.]

4. *Catechism of the Catholic Church*, 496–497.

5. Exodus 20.13.

6. Numbers 35.16–18; 1 Kings 21.19; Isaiah 1.21.

7. *Exodus: The Commentators Bible*, ed. Michael Carasik (Philadelphia: Jewish Publication Society, 2005), 162–163.

8. Wolf Gunther Plaut, *Exodus. The Torah: A Modern Commentary*, 2nd ed. (New York, 1983), 244.

9. *The Torah Anthology*, trans. Rabbi Aryek Kaplan (New York: Moznaim, 1987), 6:404. The editor takes his text from Rabbi Yaakov Culi (1689–1732). [We have been unable to locate a source that contains the English equivalent of the claim that Scola here quotes. The claim that appears in the English translation of *The Torah Anthology* is that "acts such as idolatry, Sabbath violation, and sexual crimes might be considered more sinful than murder. Still, these are crimes only against God, while murder is a crime against man."—Trans.]

10. Angelo Scola, *Buone ragioni per la vita in comune: religione, politica, economia* (Milan: Mondadori, 2010); Angelo Scola, *Una nuova laicità. Temi per una società plurale* (Venice: Marsilio, 2007), 30–31.

11. Helen Schüngel-Straumann, *Decalogo e comandamenti di Dio* (Brescia: Paideia, 1977), 49–59.

12. Brevard Childs, *The Book of Exodus: A Critical, Theological Commentary* (Philadelphia: Westminster, 1974), 385–439.

13. Childs, *The Book of Exodus*, 421.

14. André LaCocque and Paul Ricoeur, *Thinking Biblically: Exegetical and Hermeneutical Studies*, trans. David Pellauer (Chicago: University of Chicago Press, 1998). On the tension internal to the Old Testament between its tolerance of killing and the Decalogue's categorical prohibition against killing, see also Thomas

Krüger "Du sollst nicht töten!: Ehrfurcht vor dem Leben," *Zeitschrift für evangelische Ethik* 38, no. 1 (1994): 17–30. Regarding the history of the text of the Decalogue, see Innocent Himbaza, *Le Décalogue et l'histoire du texte: étude des formes textuelles du Décalogue et leurs implications dans l'histoire du texte de l'Ancien Testament* (Fribourg: Academic Press, 2004). For a rereading of the fifth commandment made by the encyclical *Evangelium Vitae*, see Brice De Malherbe, "Loi et alliance: l'obéissance au précepte 'tu ne tueras' comme expression de l'amour," in *Lo splendore della vita: vangelo, scienza ed etica*, ed. Livio Melina, Elio Sgreccia, and Stephan Kampowski (Città del Vaticano: Libreria editrice vaticana, 2006), 409–432.

15. Genesis 22.1–19.

16. Søren Kierkegaard, *Fear and Trembling; Repetition*, trans. Howard Vincent Hong and Edna Hatlestad Hong (Princeton, N.J.: Princeton University Press, 1983), 66.

17. Paul Ricoeur, " 'Thou Shalt Not Kill': A Loving Obedience," in *Thinking Biblically: Exegetical and Hermeneutical Studies*, by André LaCocque and Paul Ricoeur, trans. David Pellauer (Chicago: University of Chicago Press, 1998), 111–138.

COMMANDMENTS AND COVENANT

1. Exodus 24.7.
2. Song of Songs 1.2.

3. Deuteronomy 29.14.

4. Genesis 12.3.

5. Jeremiah 7.23.

6. [To translate Scola's use of the Italian word *appartenenza* we have, unless otherwise noted, chosen the English "belonging." The problem with this choice is that "belonging" is disloyal to the sense in which *appartenenza* implies a "part" that is, like the "part" that is part of the Italian word *appartenenza* itself, a "part of the whole." To convey this dynamic, "participation" or "partaking" would seem to be better choices but for the fact that certain disciplines of philosophy (such as set theory) have popularized the distinction between participation and belonging, where the former generally indicates a separable relation to a set and the latter an inseparable relation. Because Scola's argumentation about *appartenenza* implies a "set" that is internally indivisible and because Scola does use *partecipazione* in a separate context, it seemed unwise to render his *appartenenza* merely as "participation." Even though this choice obliterates the sense in which the "part" is literally a "part of the whole" when it comes to the Italian word *appartenenza*, there is nevertheless a sense in which this disloyalty is actually loyal in a deeper sense: in "belonging" the part is so fully a part of the whole that it disappears altogether. Ultimately, the philosophic and theological problem at issue here is the Greek word *koinonia* as it appears in Platonic political philosophy and then later in the New

Testament. *Koinonia* designates participation, community, and communion—that which is indivisibly shared and inseparably common. This is also the sense in which Scola, later in this essay, will use the terms *scomunicare* ("excommunicate") and *comunicazione* ("communication").—Trans.]

7. Exodus 20.1; 24.8.

CHRISTIANITY AND RATIONAL, UNIVERSAL MORALS

1. Here I [Angelo Scola] reiterate some thoughts I develop in "La prospettiva teologica di Veritatis splendor," in *Camminare nella luce. Prospettive della teologia morale a partire da Veritatis splendor*, ed. Livio Melina and José Noriega (Rome: Pontificia università lateranense, 2004), 65–81.

2. Scola, *Veritatis splendor*, 12–15.

3. Galatians 4.5.

4. Angelo Scola, *Questioni di antropologia teologica*, 2nd ed. (Rome: Pontificia università lateranense, 1997), 103–106.

YOU SHALL NOT KILL

1. Genesis 1.31: "God saw all he had made, and indeed it was very good."

2. Immanuel Kant, *Groundwork for the Metaphysics of Morals*, ed. and trans. Allen W. Wood (New Haven, Conn.: Yale University Press, 2002), 53–54.

3. Matthew 10.28.

4. Emmanuel Lévinas, *Totality and Infinity*, trans. Alphonso Lingis (Pittsburgh, Penn.: Duquesne University Press, 1969), 194–219.

5. [The Italian word that Scola uses here, *indisponibilità*, has no direct English equivalent. We have elected to use "indispensability" not simply because it conveys the sense of the "necessity" of every human identity but also because the English word implies several juridical forms that are consistent with Scola's argumentation. "Indispensability" is, in the first instance, "that which cannot be dispensed with." It is therefore an acceptable translation for *indisponibilità*, which in the literal sense designates "the quality of not being disposable." It also, however, has a sense in canon law, as "that which cannot admit any ecclesiastical 'dispensation,'" which is to say, any suspension or relaxation of law's strictness or consistency. It has a similar sense in common law, where it designates that which cannot be remitted, set aside, disregarded, or neglected. Last but not least, if we take the definition of property as "that which admits disposal," this translation implies that life is not property. One weakness of this translation is that Italian has a direct and clear equivalent for "indispensability" in *indispensabilità*. But because Scola does not use either *indispensabilità* or *indispensable* in his essay, the possibility for confusion is minimized.—Trans.]

6. Lévinas, *Totality and Infinity*, 198.

7. Lévinas, *Totality and Infinity*, 198.

8. Lévinas, *Totality and Infinity*, 199.

9. Lévinas, *Totality and Infinity*, 199.

10. Emmanuel Lévinas, *Difficult Freedom: Essays on Judaism*, trans. Seán Hand (Baltimore, Md.: Johns Hopkins University Press, 1990), 8.

11. Lévinas, *Difficult Freedom*, 10.

12. Lévinas, *Difficult Freedom*, 10.

13. Lévinas, *Difficult Freedom*, 10.

14. Lévinas, *Difficult Freedom*, 9.

15. See *Mekhilta de-Rabbi Ishmael*, trans. Jacob Z. Lauterbach (Lincoln: University of Nebraska Press, 2004), chap. 5. See also Emmanuel Lévinas, *In the Time of Nations*, trans. Michael B. Smith (Bloomington: Indiana University Press, 1994), 111.

16. Lévinas, *In the Time of Nations*, 189n4.

17. Theodor Adorno and Max Horkheimer, *Dialectic of Enlightenment: Philosophical Fragments*, ed. Gunzelin Schmid Noerr, trans. Edmund Jephcott (Stanford, Calif.: Stanford University Press, 2002), 6–7.

18. Michel Foucault, *The History of Sexuality*, vol. 1: *An Introduction*, trans. Robert Hurley (New York: Vintage, 1980), 135–136.

19. It is interesting, in this connection, to consider Peter Sloterdijk's provocative arguments in "Rules for the Human Zoo: A Response to the *Letter on*

Humanism," trans. Mary Rorty, *Environment and Planning D: Society and Space* 27 (2009): 12–28.

20. The manifesto was written in 1970 but first published in *The Humanist* (July/August 1974): 4–5.

RESPONSIBILITIES AND CHALLENGES: BURNING ISSUES

1. Benedict XVI, *Spe Salvi*, 1.

2. Zephaniah 3.9.

3. Livio Melina, "Riconoscere la vita. La questione epistemologica: Vangelo, scienza ed etica," in *Lo splendore della vita: vangelo, scienza ed etica*, ed. Livio Melina, Elio Sgreccia, and Stephan Kampowski (Città del Vaticano: Libreria editrice vaticana, 2006), 53–74.

4. Robert Spaemann, "Discussioni sulla vita 'degna di essere vissuta,'" *Cultura & Libri* 4, no. 27 (1987): 50 (our translation).

5. Spaemann, "Discussioni," 509. See also Robert Spaemann, *Töten oder sterben lassen? Worum es in der Euthanasiedebatte geht*, 2nd ed. (Freiburg, 1997).

6. *Evangelium Vitae*, n. 60.

7. Norman M. Ford, *When Did I Begin? Conception of the Human Individual in History, Philosophy, and Science* (Cambridge: Cambridge University Press, 1988).

8. Enrico Berti, "Quando esiste l'uomo in potenza? La tesi di Aristotele," in *Nascita e morte dell'uomo. Problemi filosofici e scientifici della bioetica*, ed. Salvino Biolo (Turin, 1993), 115–123.

9. Francis J. Beckwith and John F. Peppin, "Physician Value Neutrality: A Critique," *The Journal of Law, Medicine, and Ethics* 28, no. 1 (2000): 67–77.

10. Hans Jonas, *Potenza o impotenza della soggettività? Il problema anima-corpo quale preambolo al Principio responsabilità* (Milan, 2006).

11. Hugo Engelhardt, *The Foundations of Bioethics* (Oxford, 1986), 107.

12. Jean-Yves Goffi, "Le diagnostic prénatal et la valeur de la vie," *Studia Philosophica* 50 (1991): 107.

13. See, for example, Bernard Baertschi, "La vie humaine est-elle sacrée? Euthanasie et assistance au suicide," *Revue de Théologie et de Philosophie* 125 (1993): 359–381.

14. Peter Singer, *Practical Ethics* (Cambridge: Cambridge University Press, 1979); Peter Singer and Helga Kuhse, *Unsanctifying Human Life: Essays on Ethics* (Oxford: Blackwell, 2002).

15. Peter Singer, *Rethinking Life and Death* (Oxford: Oxford University Press, 1995), 131.

16. Peter Singer, *The Life You Can Save: Acting Now to End World Poverty* (New York: Random House, 2009); Peter Singer, "Dignity: What's So Special About Human Beings?" in *Vortrag auf der internationalen Konferenz Menschenwürde und Wissenschaft* (Heidelberg, 2004); Peter Singer, *Writings on an Ethical Life* (New York: Ecco, 2000). For an analysis of Singer's theses, see Alexander Schlegel, *Die Identität der Person. Eine Auseinandersetzung mit Peter Singer* (Freiburg, 2007).

17. Bonnie Steinbock, "Moral Status, Moral Value, and Human Embryos: Implications for Stem Cell Research," in *The Oxford Handbook of Bioethics*, ed. B. Steinbock (Oxford: Oxford University Press, 2007), 416–440.

18. Theodor Adorno and Max Horkheimer, *Dialectic of Enlightenment: Philosophical Fragments*, ed. Gunzelin Schmid Noerr, trans. Edmund Jephcott (Stanford, Calif.: Stanford University Press, 2002), xviii.

19. Adorno and Horkheimer, *Dialectic of Enlightenment*, 91.

20. Adorno and Horkheimer, *Dialectic of Enlightenment*, 91.

21. Carlo Viano, "Uccidere è lecito," *Rivista di Filosofia* 88, no. 2 (1997): 315–321. See also Adriano Pessina, *Eutanasia: della morte e di altre cose* (Siena, 2007).

22. *Das medizinisch assistierte Sterben: Zur Sterbehilfe aus medizinischer, ethischer, juristischer und theologischer Sicht*, ed. Adrian Holderegger (Freiburg, 1999). Especially crude is Jacob Appel's thesis on the problem of the legitimization of suicide for the mentally disabled in Switzerland. See "A Suicide Right for the Mentally Ill? A Swiss Case Opens a New Debate," *Hastings Center Report* 37, no. 3 (2007): 21–23.

23. Immanuel Kant, *Groundwork for the Metaphysics of Morals*, ed. and trans. Allen W. Wood (New Haven, Conn.: Yale University Press, 2002), 54.

24. Angel Rodríguez-Luño, "Valore e senso della vita: la responsabilità etica," in *Lo splendore della vita: vangelo, scienza ed etica*, ed. Livio Melina, Elio Sgreccia, and Stephan Kampowski (Città del Vaticano: Libreria editrice vaticana, 2006), 99–108.

25. Emmanuel Lévinas, *Ethics and Infinity: Conversations with Phillipe Nemo*, trans. Richard A. Cohen (Pittsburgh, Penn.: Duquesne University Press, 1985), 86–87.

26. Robert Spaemann, *Persone. Sulla differenza tra qualcosa e qualcuno* (Rome-Bari, 2007).

27. Juan-José Pérez-Soba, "La vita personale: fra il dono e la donazione," in *Lo splendore della vita: vangelo, scienza ed etica*, ed. Livio Melina, Elio Sgreccia, and Stephan Kampowski (Città del Vaticano: Libreria editrice vaticana, 2006), 127–144.

28. Gabriel Marcel, *Homo Viator: Introduction to a Metaphysics of Hope*, trans. Emma Craufurd (New York: Harper, 1962), 84.

29. Gianni Angelini, "La vita: fatto o promessa? L'etica come fedeltà alla vita," *Rivista di Teologia Morale* 71 (1986): 55–69; Gianni Angelini, "Non uccidere: per una rinnovata comprensione del quinto comandamento," *Rivista di Teologia Morale* 72 (1986): 33–48.

30. Martin Rhonheimer, *La prospettiva della morale. Fondamenti dell'etica filosofica* (Roma, 1994), 280–288. For this argument, see also Livio Melina, "Gli assoluti

della morale in discussione," in *Morale: tra crisi e rinnovamento* (Milano, 1993), 41–61.

31. Alberto Bonandi, "Suicidio come omicidio e ritorno," *Teologia* 31 (2006): 36–74.

32. Giuseppe Angelini, "L'eutanasia: tra desiderio di morire e fuga dalla morte," *Rivista del Clero Italiano* 10 (1985): 664–671.

33. Angelo Scola, *Morte e libertà* (Siena, 2004); Livio Melina, "Eutanasia o Eucaristia? Dalla retorica della 'buona morte' al morire con Cristo," *Communio* 145 (1996): 57–67.

34. Benedict XVI, *Spe Salvi*, 27.

A SPECIAL LAW

A1. Emmanuel Levinas, "From Ethics to Exegesis," in *In the Time of the Nations*, trans. Michael B. Smith (Bloomington: Indiana University Press, 1994), 111.

2. [Throughout her essay Cavarero deliberately uses *uomo* as a generic term for the human beings whose civilization she is discussing, and we have carefully and consistently translated her *uomo* as "man." To render her *uomo* in a less clearly gendered terminology would be to undermine Cavarero's rhetorical strategy and intention.—Trans.]

3. John Locke, *Two Treatises on Government, and a Letter Concerning Toleration*, ed. Ian Shapiro (New Haven, Conn.: Yale University Press, 2003), 104.

1. Matthew 19.18; Mark 10.19; Luke 18.20.

1. [Cavarero's reference to "*il potere costituito*" invokes Emmanuel Joseph Sieyès's distinction between *pouvoir constituant*, the power to call a juridical order into being (through revolution, for example), and *pouvoirs constitués*, the powers exercised by an already existing juridical order (such as, for example, the powers of a sitting legislature).—Trans.]

2. Cyprian, "To Donatus," trans. Robert Ernest Wallis, in *Ante-Nicene Fathers: Translations of The Writings of the Fathers down to AD 325*, ed. Alexander Roberts, James Donaldson, and A. Cleveland Coxe (Buffalo, N.Y.: Christian Literature Publishing Co., 1886), 5:277.

3. Theodor Adorno, "Cultural Criticism and Society," in *Prisms*, trans. Samuel Weber and Shierry Weber (Cambridge, Mass.: The MIT Press, 1967), 34.

4. Hannah Arendt, *Origins of Totalitarianism* (New York: Harcourt, Brace & Jovanovich, 1973), 443.

5. For the significance of this neologism and for the thesis developed in this paragraph, see my *Horrorism: Naming Contemporary Violence*, trans. William McCuaig (New York: Columbia University Press, 2009).

1. See, on this point, Jan Assmann, *Non avrai altro Dio. Il Monoteismo e il linguaggio della violenza* (Bologna: Il Mulino, 2007).

2. Exodus 32.27–28.

3. Deuteronomy 20.16.

4. Exodus 20.5; Deuteronomy 5.9.

5. See, on this point, Norbert Lohfink, *Il Dio della Bibbia e la violenza* (Brescia, 1985).

6. Franco Volpi with Antonio Gnoli, *Il Decalogo. Onora il padre e la madre* (Milan, 2008), 33 (our translation).

7. See, on this point, among others, Roland Herbert Bainton, *Il Cristiano, la guerra e la pace* (Turin, 1968); Emilio Butturini, *La croce e lo scettro* (Fiesole, 1990); Dag Tessore, *La mistica della guerra* (Roma, 2003). For a survey of other themes that I take up below, see Marco Geuna, "Le relazioni fra gli Stati e il problema della guerra: alcuni modelli teorici da Vitoria a Hume," in *La pace e le guerre: guerra giusta e filosofie della pace*, ed. Annamaria Loche (Cagliari, 2005), 45–130.

8. Jessica Stern, *Terror in the Name of God* (New York: Harper Perennial, 2004); Mark Juergensmeyer, *Terroristi in nome di Dio. La violenza religiosa nel mondo* (Roma-Bari, 2003).

9. Thomas Aquinas, *Political Writings*, ed. and trans. Robert W. Dyson (Cambridge: Cambridge University

Press, 2002), 239–266. See especially IIaIIae 40 ("On War") and IIaIIae 64 ("On Homicide").

10. Lohfink, *Il Dio della Bibbia e la violenza*, 20.

11. Michael Walzer, *Just and Unjust Wars* (New York: Basic Books, 1978); Michael Walzer, *Arguing About War* (New Haven, Conn.: Yale University Press, 2004). See also Jeff McMahan, "The Ethics of Killing in War," *Philosophia* 34 (2006): 23–41.

TO CUT LIFE SHORT

1. Genesis 4.10.

2. Genesis 9.7.

3. Hannah Arendt, *The Human Condition* (Chicago: University of Chicago Press, 1958), 315.

4. Arendt, *The Human Condition*, 315.

5. Arendt, *The Human Condition*, 321.

6. For the categories of "naked life" and "biopolitics" that are today the object of a vast critical literature, the paradigmatic text is Giorgio Agamben, *Homo Sacer: Sovereign Power and Bare Life*, trans. Daniel Heller-Roazen (Stanford, Calif.: Stanford University Press, 1998).

7. See, on this point, Davide Tarizzo, *La vita, un'invenzione recente* (Roma-Bari, 2010).

8. For a collection devoted to this theme, see Giovanni Fornero, *Bioetica cattolica e bioetica laica. Con un postscritto 2009* (Milan, 2009).

9. Augustine, *De Civitate Dei*, trans. Patrick Gerard Walsh (Oxford: Oxbow, 2005), 71.

10. Ecclesiastes 3.2.

11. On this very complex question, see the special issue of *Filosofia politica* devoted to the problem of the "quality of life," in particular Simona Forti's editorial, "La vita e le sue qualità ai tempi del biopotere," *Filosofia politica* 23, no. 3 (2009): 353–363.

12. Arendt, *The Human Condition*, 315.

13. See Stefano Rodotà, *La vita e le regole* (Milan, 2009), 251.

14. Hans Kung and Walter Jens, *Della dignità del morire* (Milan, 2010).

15. Roberta De Monticelli, *Sullo spirito e l'ideologia. Lettera ai cristiani* (Milan, 2007), 39.

A WEAK COMMANDMENT

1. See, on this point, Gustavo Zagrebelsky, *Contro l'etica della verità* (Rome-Bari, 2009).

IN THE BEGINNING

1. Leo Strauss, "Jerusalem and Athens," in *Jewish Philosophy and the Crisis of Modernity: Essays and Lectures in Modern Jewish Thought*, ed. Kenneth Hart Green (Albany, N.Y.: SUNY Press, 1997), 377–408.

2. Jean-Pierre Vernant and Pierre Vidal-Naquet, *Myth and Tragedy in Ancient Greece*, trans. Janet Lloyd (New York: Zone, 1998), 298.

3. See Eva Cantarella, *Studi sull'omicidio in di- ritto greco e romano* (Milan, 1976); Eva Cantarella, "Private Revenge and Public Justice," *Punishment and Society* 3 (2001): 472–482.

4. Homer, *Iliad*, trans. Barry Powell (Oxford: Oxford University Press, 2014), XVI 351–355.

5. Deuteronomy 19.21.

6. Plato *Laws* 864b.

7. Émile Benveniste, *Indo-European Language and Society*, trans. Elizabeth Palmer (Miami: University of Miami Press, 1973), 426.

8. Elias Canetti, *Crowds and Power*, trans. Carol Stewart (New York: Farrar, Straus and Giroux, 1984), 67–68.

HOMO NECANS

1. Walter Burkert, *Homo Necans* (Berkeley: University of California Press, 1983).

2. See, respectively, Melanie Klein, Konrad Lorenz, and René Girard.

3. Erasmus, *Dulce bellum inexpertis* (1515).

4. Thomas Hobbes, *On the Citizen*, ed. and trans. Richard Tuck (Cambridge: Cambridge University Press, 1998), 102.

5. Emmanuel Lévinas, "Peace and Proximity," in *Alterity and Transcendence*, trans. Michael B. Smith (London: Athlone, 1999), 131.

6. Fyodor Dostoevsky, *The Brothers Karamazov*, trans. Richard Pevear and Larissa Volokhonsky (New York: Farrar, Straus and Giroux, 2002), 224.

YOU SHALL NEVER KILL

1. Emmanuel Lévinas, "Peace and Proximity," in *Alterity and Transcendence*, trans. Michael B. Smith (London: Athlone, 1999), 136.

2. Emmanuel Lévinas, "From Ethics to Exegesis," in *In the Time of the Nations*, trans. Michael B. Smith (Bloomington: Indiana University Press, 1994), 111.

3. Emmanuel Lévinas, *Totality and Infinity: An Essay on Exteriority*, trans. Alphonso Lingis (Pittsburgh, Penn.: Duquesne University Press, 1969), 23.

4. Emmanuel Lévinas, *Difficult Freedom: Essays on Judaism*, trans. Séan Hand (Baltimore, Md.: Johns Hopkins University Press, 1990), 19–20.

5. Lévinas, *Difficult Freedom*, 211.

6. Matthew 19.19; Luke 19.18.

7. Matthew 5.44.

8. Emmanuel Lévinas, *Alterity and Transcendence*, trans. Michael B. Smith (New York: Columbia University Press, 1999), 141–142.

1. Jacques Derrida, *Politics of Friendship*, trans. George Collins (New York: Verso, 1997), 156. Translation modified.

2. Norberto Elias, *The Civilizing Process*, trans. Edmund Jephcott (Malden, Mass.: Blackwell, 2000).

3. Giovanni De Luna, *Il corpo del nemico ucciso* (Turin, 2006), 288.

4. De Luna, *Il corpo*, 288.

5. De Luna, *Il corpo*, 288.

6. Sophocles, *Antigone*, trans. Richard Emile Braun (Oxford: Oxford University Press, 1974), 42.

7. Virginia Woolf, *Three Guineas* (Orlando, Fla.: Harcourt, 1966), 6.

8. For the major representative of this critical vein, see Judith Butler, *Precarious Life: The Powers of Mourning and Violence* (New York: Verso, 2004), 19–49. I am obliged to refer again to my *Horrorism: Naming Contemporary Violence*, trans. William McCuaig (New York: Columbia University Press, 2009). For a reflection on these positions, see *Differenza e relazione. L'ontologia dell'umano nel pensiero di Judith Butler e Adriana Cavarero*, ed. Lorenzo Bernini and Olivia Guaraldo (Verona: Ombre Corte, 2009).

INDEX

Miguel Vatter, *The Republic of the Living: Biopolitics and the Critique of Civil Society.*

Maurizio Ferraris, *Where Are You? An Ontology of the Cell Phone.* Translated by Sarah De Sanctis.

Irving Goh, *The Reject: Community, Politics, and Religion after the Subject.*

Kevin Attell, *Giorgio Agamben: Beyond the Threshold of Deconstruction.*

J. Hillis Miller, *Communities in Fiction.*

Remo Bodei, *The Life of Things, the Love of Things.* Translated by Murtha Baca.

Gabriela Basterra, *The Subject of Freedom: Kant, Levinas.*

Roberto Esposito, *Categories of the Impolitical.* Translated by Connal Parsley.

Roberto Esposito, *Two: The Machine of Political Theology and the Place of Thought.* Translated by Zakiya Hanafi.

Akiba Lerner, *Redemptive Hope: From the Age of Enlightenment to the Age of Obama.*

Adriana Cavarero and Angelo Scola, *Thou Shalt Not Kill: A Political and Theological Dialogue.* Translated by Margaret Adams Groesbeck and Adam Sitze.

Massimo Cacciari, *Europe and Empire: On the Political Forms of Globalization.* Edited by Alessandro Carrera, Translated by Massimo Verdicchio.

Emanuele Coccia, *Sensible Life: A Micro-ontology of the Image.* Translated by Scott Stuart, Introduction by Kevin Attell.